THE BABY COOKBOOK

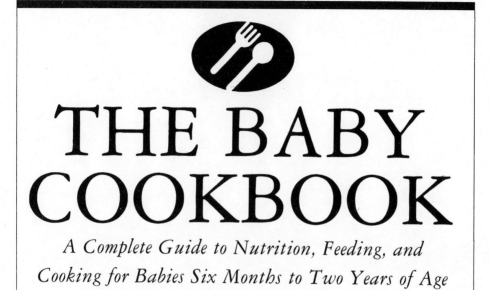

THE BABY COOKBOOK

A Complete Guide to Nutrition, Feeding, and
Cooking for Babies Six Months to Two Years of Age

Karin Knight, R.N.
Jeannie Lumley

WILLIAM MORROW AND COMPANY, INC.

New York

Library of Congress Cataloging in Publication Data

Knight, Karin.
  The baby cookbook.

  Bibliography: p.
  Includes indexes.
  1. Cookery (Baby foods) 2. Infants—Nutrition.
I. Lumley, Jeannie. II. Title.
TX740.K59 1985   649'.3   84-25438
ISBN 0-688-04168-X
ISBN 0-688-04950-8 (pbk.)

Printed in the United States of America

First Edition

1 2 3 4 5 6 7 8 9 10

BOOK DESIGN BY KAROLINA HARRIS

To my beloved Baba Muktananda

K. K.

Foreword

FROM a practical standpoint, the feeding of infants and young children presents a number of challenges to the young parent of the 1980s. Our society has changed from the days of the close family unit, when experienced grandparents were available to give counsel. Young couples are left primarily to "on the job training" in deciding what is best in child rearing. Good pediatric care and evaluation, with advice on such basic information as healthy nutrition, can be costly or unavailable for many parents. Unfortunately, even where such care is available, many times a good, healthy nutritional program is not a major part of the care provided.

We have come to new understandings of the importance of healthy nutrition in recent years. More and more young parents are seeking to learn how best to feed their children and to provide models of good eating habits themselves.

The Baby Cookbook is a valuable, readable guide to basic nutritional facts, set in the context of feeding an infant from the introduction of early solids at approximately six months of age to the time of independent self-feeding and diet selection by the age of two years. Both the principles of sound nutrition and a reasonable, practical approach to when, how, and what to offer a child at each stage of his development are covered. The progression from puréed to more coarse (junior texture) foods, through to soft table foods and finger-feeding of small pieces of table foods is appropriately detailed. The many recipes, which can be prepared, stored, and served by the busy parent inexpensively and conveniently, make this book a complete, practical guide to feeding children during their first two years.

With this book Karin Knight and Jeannie Lumley have made a significant contribution to parents and their young children, and they have provided as well a referral source for physicians in this important area of good nutrition. Equally valuable is their approach to the hows and whys of developing good patterns and habits of feeding, which are often so difficult for young parents to establish.

H. JAMES HOLROYD, M.D., F.A.A.P.
Clinical Professor of Pediatrics
University of Southern California
School of Medicine

Foreword

The Baby Cookbook is an excellent resource for new parents who are faced with the task of providing a healthy diet for their children. Karin Knight has sorted through the myriad of nutrition myths and misconceptions to compile a concise, accurate, and informative handbook on the hows and whys of nourishing an infant and toddler.

The thoughts recorded in the diary section will help parents reflect on the challenges they face at each stage of the child's development.

A wide selection of low-salt, low-sugar recipes offers many inspirations to end the "What shall I cook today?" doldrums. There are numerous recipes that the whole family will enjoy, and they wisely incorporate foods from many cultures. Exposing the young child to a variety of foods will help to mold healthy eating patterns which should last a lifetime.

LINDA BROWN, R.D., M.P.H.
Chief Clinical Dietitian
Children's Hospital of Los Angeles

Acknowledgments

SINCERE thanks to the following people for their professional expertise, time, and resources: Linda Brown, R.D., M.P.H.; H. James Holroyd, M.D.; Harvey Hammond, Chief Librarian, Children's Hospital of Los Angeles; Nina Dudenhoeffer, R.D.; Wayne Herbert, M.D.; and to our agent, Sue Zeckendorf, and editors Elizabeth Knappman and Narcisse Chamberlain.

Love and thanks also go to our wonderful families and friends, who shared our enthusiasm and everyday chores so that we could write this book.

And special thanks to Bob, William, Robert, Roz, Chris, Tom, Karin Krogsrud, Randye West, Elissa Fleiss, Benita Brazier, and Jana Hunter for their support, critiques, and recipe ideas.

K. K. AND J. L.

Contents

PART 1
NUTRITION AND FEEDING GUIDE
FROM SIX MONTHS TO TWO YEARS

PART 2
FAMILY RECIPES
AND SPECIAL CHILDREN'S RECIPES

Introduction

YOU are probably reading *The Baby Cookbook* because you are a new parent, or else you are expecting a baby. And you are obviously anxious to do the best possible job in raising a happy, healthy child. A couple of years ago I too found that I was pregnant. As I was over forty and had two late-teenage sons, my husband, Bob, and I had been dreaming of some peace around the house and a little time to relax. This obviously wasn't meant to be. After some serious readjustments in our thinking, and time to get used to the idea, we were elated. Our daughter, Mirabai, has brought us more joy than we could have imagined.

I wanted the very best for my little girl, just as I had for my sons. Twenty years ago I knew little about raising babies and infant nutrition. With a lot of love and work, the boys grew up just fine, but there were many times when I wished I could turn back the clock and use the knowledge I later gained. I would have done many things differently. With Mirabai's arrival I felt I had been given that chance. After reading many books on child care and psychology, I searched for good books on infant nutrition and cooking for babies. Not finding what I was looking for, I decided to write *The Baby Cookbook*. It contains much more than just how to cook for a baby. My aim has been to provide a complete feeding guide, in the context of family life.

My work as a public health nurse has made me extremely aware of the importance of a nutritious diet, not only for childhood development but also for good health in maturity. In observing Mirabai, I was amazed to see how quickly both good and bad eating habits were formed. The younger she was the easier it was to encourage good habits. After some research, and with this in mind, I decided that six months was the optimum age to start introducing solids. This is where *The Baby Cookbook* begins.

The first chapter on the technical facts of nutrition may not be the easiest reading in the world. However, it is important to understanding the rest of the book, which is much more fun and will, I hope, show you how to apply what I have learned: that a healthy diet, combined with a happy attitude toward mealtimes, will give your baby a good start in life.

My apologies for referring to all babies in my book as "he." This is done only for simplification. In the same way, the term "father" may be read in place of "mother" (except in the case of breast-feeding, of course!) for all the many fathers who are equally concerned about their children's physical well-being.

There are several points that I should emphasize to you:

· This is a well-baby book. If you are in any doubt whatsoever about your baby's health, you should consult a physician.
· Although I recommend starting solids at six months of age, all babies have individual needs. Some may be ready at four months, while others may still be mainly breast-fed at one year. You and your pediatrician are the best people to decide when the right time comes for your baby.
· Your observations and instincts about your own child are usually the best. The information in this book should be used with that in mind.

I hope you enjoy *The Baby Cookbook*, especially Mirabai's diary at the conclusion of Part I. It shares not only my daughter's reactions to new foods and experiences, but also my whole family's interactions with her. Part II, Family Recipes, includes recipes devised especially for her, but it also illustrates how I have been cooking for the entire family since Mirabai started on solid foods. She can be served a spoonful of almost everything in our adult meals now. We all consider our diets much more consciously, we are a trimmer family, and—a wonderful bonus—my youngest son has given up being a junk-food addict.

KARIN KNIGHT, R.N.

THE BABY COOKBOOK

NUTRITION
AND FEEDING GUIDE
FROM SIX MONTHS
TO TWO YEARS

Nutrition and Nutrients
—Their Importance
to Babies

SAGES have said that food nourishes and protects, and food destroys. Food is life, and food is disease. What we consume should refine our intellect, give us inner peace, keep our mind and body strong, and enable us to function beautifully in life. What better could we want for our babies?

The sages and science seem to think alike here. Most of our illnesses are diet related, especially congestive heart failure, cancer, diabetes, strokes, and heart attacks. Good nutrition will give us good health if we also have a happy, healthy attitude toward our diet and our body. Love, happiness, laughter, and caring—all need to be added to a nutritious diet for total well-being.

Most of us think of diet and nutrition as the same thing. However, diet is the food and liquids we consume (some of which the body uses and some of which go to waste), and nutrition is the process by which the body utilizes what we eat and drink. Food supplies the raw materials for growth and energy. It allows the body to pursue its complicated process of metabolism. All living cells require a multitude of nutrients and may become malnourished if even one essential ingredient is lacking.

Good nutrition is required for normal development in all children. It also helps maintain the body's natural defense system, which in turn helps the body resist infections. To achieve good nutrition, our bodies need an adequate and balanced amount of protein, fats, carbohydrates, vitamins, and minerals.

A well baby is born with a vibrant, healthy body. As new parents, it is one of our primary duties to maintain our children's good health. The foundations for your baby's future well-being are being laid now, and during these early years you will have the pleasure of watching him develop through one of the most exciting and crucial growth periods of his life. I hope the following pages will help make the experience a joyful and healthy one for both of you.

PROTEINS

Proteins are invaluable. They are necessary for tissue maintenance and repair. They help build blood and antibodies to fight infection and are an important source of energy. They aid healthy digestion and are essential for proper elimination of waste material. A lack of protein may cause a craving for sweets and starches, and protein malnutrition can cause permanent stunting of physical growth, failure to reach full intellectual development, and susceptibility to infectious diseases.

Since the chief function of proteins is to supply the body with building materials, they can be thought of as "building blocks"—in nutritional language, amino acids. The human body is capable of manufacturing fourteen of these amino acids, which are referred to as "nonessential" because they need not be obtained from specific dietary sources. Certain amino acids cannot be manufactured by the body itself, or cannot be formed at a sufficiently rapid rate to meet the body's demands, and are called "essential" amino acids. There are eight of them—lysine, leucine, isoleucine, methionine, tryptophan, threonine, valine, and phenylalanine—all of which must be obtained from food sources.

There are two additional amino acids, histidine and arginine, which may also be called essential for children, as their bodies cannot produce them fast enough to ensure an adequate supply. Both are plentiful in cheese, milk, and eggs.

A "complete protein" must contain all these essential amino acids, the best food sources for which are meat, fish, poultry, eggs, cheese, and milk.

Other foods contain some amino acids but not all, and these foods are called "incomplete proteins." Peas, most kinds of beans, rice, cereals, lentils, and processed flour all provide incomplete proteins. However, if different kinds of incomplete proteins are combined, excellent sources of high complete protein can be created (see table below). However, a few points should be kept in mind:

· The importance of knowing which foods complement others. (Sometimes information is limited on amino acid content.)
· A larger quantity of food is necessary to supply adequate amounts of protein from incomplete-protein sources, and children's stomachs and appetites are small.
· A well-balanced meal combining beans and rice, tofu and rice, or beans and pasta will not be adequate if a child will eat only one of the two foods.
· Two or more incomplete proteins *must* be eaten at the same time. Lentils for lunch and rice pudding for dinner do not provide a complete protein.

When incomplete proteins are combined, not only should foods that supplement limited amino acids be included, they should be combined in proportion to each other for the most efficient utilization of protein. The ratio is specific for each combination. Some examples are:

¾ cup dry rice in combination with ¼ cup dry beans
¾ cup dry rice in combination with 1 cup milk or ¼ cup milk powder
3¼ cups wheat flour in combination with ¼ cup soy grits and ½ cup sesame seeds

Complementation of proteins is also a practical way to enhance the value of foods readily accepted by young children. For example, some ways of accomplishing this are by adding a small amount of soy grits to oatmeal while cooking, or adding wheat germ, soy flour, and dry milk to muffins, pancakes, and breads.

A simple method, called the Cornell Triple Rich Flour Formula, developed at Cornell University, complements the proteins in baked goods. Before flour is measured, the following ingredients should go into the bottom of each cup:

> 1 tbsp. soy flour
> 1 tbsp. dry milk
> 1 tsp. wheat germ

Then the flour is added to the desired amount.

As essential as protein is to the body's well-being, it is important to remember that if a child is put on a restricted diet, such as a vegetarian diet, there is a danger of an inadequate protein supply. A pure vegetarian (vegan) diet eliminates all animal foods, thus removing all concentrated sources of protein, calcium, and vitamin B_{12}. A lacto-ovo vegetarian diet eliminates all meat from the general diet, but includes eggs, milk, and other dairy products. Some lacto-ovo vegetarian diets may include fish and occasionally poultry. Based on individual food choices, a lacto-ovo vegetarian diet can be adequate in all nutrients. For the young child, however, it is difficult to provide sufficient quality and quantity of proteins in the diet, and an adequate amount of calories and minerals to support normal growth, without including dairy products or eggs.

No extreme diet should be undertaken without first consulting a doctor and having a complete understanding of what is involved.

FATS

Most of us should cut down on the amount of fat we consume. We do, however, need a certain amount of fat for good health. Fats

TABLE OF INCOMPLETE PROTEINS	
For quality protein from vegetable sources, use a food from Column I only in combination with a food from Column II.	
Column I	*Column II*
Legumes	Beans: *adzuki*, black, fava, kidney, lima, marrow, mung, navy, pea, pinto, soy (tofu)	Dairy products (milk, eggs, yogurt, cheese, cottage cheese) Grains
Grains	Whole grains: barley, corn (corn bread), grits, oats, rice, rye, wheat (bulgur, wheat germ), sprouts	Nuts and seeds Dairy products Legumes
Nuts and Seeds	Nuts: almonds, beechnuts, Brazil nuts, cashews, filberts, pecans, pine nuts, walnuts Seeds: pumpkin, sunflower	Dairy products Legumes

TABLE OF RECOMMENDED DAILY DIETARY ALLOWANCES FOR PROTEIN, 1980*						
	Weight		*Height*		*Energy*	*Protein*
	(kg.)	*(lb.)*	*(cm.)*	*(in.)*	*(kcal.)*	*(g.)*
Infants 0.5–1 yr.	9	20	71	28	kg x 105	kg x 2.0
Children 1–3 yrs.	13	29	90	35	1300	23

Legend: kg. = kilogram   1 kg. = 2.2 lbs.   1 lb. = .45 kg.
cm. = centimeter   1 cm. = 0.39 inch 1 inch = 2.54 cm.
kcal. = 1,000 calories
g. = gram   1 g. = .035 ounce 1 ounce = 28.35 g.

*Source: *Recommended Dietary Allowances*, Food and Nutrition Board, National Academy of Sciences, National Research Council, Washington, D.C.

contain nutritional components called essential fatty acids that are necessary to proper growth and without which we may develop rashes, scaling skin, and hair loss.

Fat is a component of every cell in the body and serves a number of important functions. It acts as a storage depot for energy and other nutrients, is a conductor of heat, and serves very well as insulation against temperature extremes. Our kidneys are protected from injury by the fat that surrounds them.

On a practical level, fats take longer to digest than other foods, help us feel full, and give certain foods their distinctive tastes and aromas. (Just think of the delicious smell of onions fried in butter!)

Fats also carry the fat-soluble vitamins A, D, E, and K. If we cut out fat in our diets, we also knock out the nutrients that travel with them, and this, carried to extremes, would result in vitamin deficiencies. As there are plenty of meats and vegetables containing fats, a varied diet will prevent this from happening. Some other sources of fat are butter, margarine, vegetable oils, egg yolk, nuts, cheese, mayonnaise, peanut butter, whole milk, and cream.

For health reasons, dietary fats should be kept to a minimum, especially the saturated fats. Food products from land animals generally contain saturated fat, as do a few from vegetable origin, such as coconut, coconut oil, and palm kernel oil, which are found in commercial cookies, cake mixes, and nondairy sour cream and whipped toppings. Saturated fats tend to raise the level of cholesterol in the blood and (together with inherited genes) are the villains in arteriosclerosis and heart disease.

Oils of vegetable origin, such as corn, cottonseed, safflower, sesame, soybean, and sunflower seed, are polyunsaturated and best to use for cooking and salads.

There are certain monounsaturated fats that do not raise or lower the cholesterol level. These are called "neutral fats." Olive oil, peanut oil, peanut butter, avocados, and nuts (except walnuts, which contain polyunsaturated oil) are primarily neutral in their fat content.

Excess fat in the diet is better replaced with carbohydrates such as whole-grain breads and cereals, fruits, vegetables, and potatoes. These foods provide vitamins, minerals, and fiber (nature's laxative) as well as calories.

CARBOHYDRATES

Carbohydrates are a controversial subject in nutrition today. They are, however, essential in providing energy and are basically the body's raw fuel. When ingested, some carbohydrates, in the form of glucose, are used for immediate energy needs, some are stored in the liver and muscles, and the remainder are converted to fat. An important function of carbohydrates is to spare proteins from having to supply body energy, leaving them to fulfill the proteins' role in building and repairing body tissue.

Carbohydrates are divided into two groups: *simple carbohydrates* and *complex carbohydrates*. The first group contains sugars and the second contains starches, which also supply bulk and fiber.

The three simple carbohydrates are glucose, fructose, and galactose. Glucose is moderately sweet and, although found in a few foods such as corn syrup, it is chiefly produced in the body by digested starches. All other forms of sugar are converted by the body into glucose. Fructose is found in fruit and honey, and galactose is made in the body by digested lactose (milk sugar).

Carbohydrates also contain "double sugars," the three primary ones being sucrose, lactose, and maltose. Sucrose is common table sugar (large amounts of which have been linked to increased dental cavities in infants and children). It is found in many food sources, including cane and beet sugars, sorghum, molasses, and maple syrup. Small amounts of sucrose occur naturally in most fruits and many vegetables.

Lactose is the sugar found in milk and is the major dietary carbohydrate consumed by infants.

Maltose occurs in malt products and germinated cereals.

The complex carbohydrates include starches, dextrin, cellulose, pectin, and other forms of fiber. Starch is by far the most important of these and accounts for about half the total carbohydrate intake in the American diet. In many other countries starch is the staple food, making up an even higher proportion of the total diet.

Cellulose and other fibers are not digested by the human body, but remain in the digestive tract, contributing important bulk to the diet. This bulk helps move the digested food mass through the system. The main sources of cellulose are stems and leaves of vegetables, seeds, and grain coverings and hulls.

The best food sources for carbohydrates are breads, cereals, flour products, noodles and pasta, grains and rice, potatoes, peas, beans, vegetables, and fruits.

FIBER

Fiber has recently been of great public interest, following indications that it might help prevent certain diseases such as colon cancer, obesity, coronary heart disease, diverticulitis, and irritable bowel syndrome, all of which have been at least partially linked to low-fiber, high-cholesterol, and high-saturated-fat diets.

Fiber is the part of food that resists digestion in the human gastrointestinal tract. It is found only in plants (not in the sinewy parts of meats, as is sometimes believed).

There are two different terms used in reference to fiber: *crude fiber* and *dietary fiber*. This can cause confusion when trying to estimate the amount of fiber contained in a specific product, but the fiber content listed on packages usually refers to crude fiber. *Crude fiber* is the food material (consisting primarily of cellulose) that remains after the food has gone through the digestive process.

Dietary fiber includes more substances than crude fiber. It is a mixture of complex carbohydrates that are largely resistant to human digestion, such as cellulose, hemicellulose, pectin, and a noncarbohydrate called lignin.* Crude-fiber analysis does not accurately reflect the entire amount of dietary fiber in food products. It apparently represents only one fifth to one half the total dietary fiber present in food.

*Pectin is, however, one fiber substance that is digested.

Although the physiological effects of dietary fiber are not completely understood, increased amounts of fiber in the diet result in decreased intestinal transit time, increased stool-water content, and, in certain circumstances, a reduction in cholesterol.

Unfortunately, most of the research performed on the benefits of fiber relates to adults. Now the important question is, should fiber in the diet of infants, toddlers, and children be increased? If so, this would necessitate an increase in the consumption of fruits, vegetables, legumes, and whole-grain cereals and breads. A recent study showed that a large percentage of children eat less than the recommended daily amounts of fruits and vegetables, breads, and cereals; that 50 percent of those studied ate one or less fruits or vegetables high in vitamin C each day; and that 30 percent to 40 percent of one- to five-year-olds receive less than two thirds the recommended daily allowance of vitamin C. This would indicate that there *is* a need for children to increase their intake of fiber-containing foods.

However, some objections have been made to increasing fiber in a child's diet. One reason is that a child has a limited stomach capacity. High-fiber foods are low in calories but high in bulk, thereby diminishing the child's ability to receive an adequate caloric intake. Another objection is that dietary fiber may adversely influence the absorption of certain essential minerals, such as calcium, iron, copper, magnesium, phosphorus, and zinc. Insufficient research has been done to confirm or reject this theory at this time, but the American Academy of Pediatrics feels that a substantial amount of fiber should probably be consumed to ensure normal laxation.

It seems unlikely that fiber is necessary for babies less than twelve months old, but with the introduction of solid foods into the diets of older children, care should be taken to include whole-grain breads, cereals, fruits, and vegetables. However, a diet that places emphasis on high-fiber, low-calorie foods, to the exclusion of the other common food groups, would not be recommended for children.

The following table shows the fiber content of common foods, as well as portions that should be served to one- to three-year-olds:

FIBER CONTENT OF FOODS (per 100 mg)*		
Food	Little Fiber (0.2 gm)	Low Fiber (0.5 gm; range 0.3–1 gm)
Bread	White, cracked wheat, rye, pumpernickel breads; white crackers	Whole wheat bread and crackers
Cereals	Rice, macaroni, noodles, spaghetti	Barley, Cheerios, cornflakes, farina, oatmeal, puffed rice, brown rice, shredded wheat, Wheaties
Vegetables		Asparagus, beets, cabbage, carrots, celery, collards, corn, cucumbers, eggplant, lettuce, mushrooms, onions, sweet potato, white potato with or without skin, summer squash, spinach, tomato, white turnip
Fruits	Juices only	Applesauce, apricots, banana, canned fruit cocktail, grapes, cherries, grapefruit, mango, melon, oranges, papaya, pears without skin, pineapple, plums, prunes, raisins, rhubarb

Moderate Fiber (1.5 gm; range 1.1–2.0 gm)	High Fiber (3 gm; range 2.1–4.2 gm)	Serving size for 1–3 yrs.
		½ slice of bread 4 servings
40% bran flakes, puffed wheat, raisin bran	All-Bran (4.8 gm/cup), wheat germ (2.5 gm/cup)	½ oz (½ cup) ready-to-eat cereal; ¼ cup cooked cereal or pasta 4 servings
Green and wax beans, dried beans and peas (kidney, lima, lentils, split pea, soybeans, etc.); broccoli; Brussels sprouts; cauliflower; dandelion, kale and mustard greens; fresh or frozen green peas; okra, parsnip, peppers, pumpkin, rutabaga, winter squash	Artichoke, 1 large (2.4 gm); green peas canned only (2.3 gm/½ cup)	¼ cup 2 servings or more
Apples, avocado, berries except blackberries, figs, fresh pears with skin	Fresh blackberries (4.1 gm/¾ cup), dried figs (5.6 gm/cup), dried dates (2.3 gm/½ cup)	¼ cup fruit; ¼ cup juice 2 servings or more; fruits with pits not advised

*From *Diet Manual Massachusetts General Hospital*, Little, Brown, Boston, 1976. Fiber values assigned are based on data in *Composition of Foods—Raw, Processed, Prepared* (Agricultural Handbook No. 8), Bernice K. Watt, and Annabel L. Merrill, U.S. Department of Agriculture, Agricultural Research Service, Washington, D.C., 1963.

VITAMINS

The word "vitamin" means living substance. Vitamins are organic compounds, essential for proper utilization of food and healthy functioning of the body. They have been referred to as invisible helpers, ready to aid in building and maintaining a perfect body. However, the body cannot manufacture vitamins, so it must receive them through food. Each vitamin performs a special function and, although only small quantities are required, a serious deficiency of any one could prove disastrous. A well-balanced diet will supply adequate amounts of all the vitamins.

Vitamin pills are not intended to be, and should not be used as, a substitute for vitamin foods. However, if a child's appetite is poor or his eating habits so bad that he is not getting a balanced diet, fat-soluble and water-soluble vitamins may be added. But remember that vitamins cannot compensate for a diet lacking in fats, proteins, and carbohydrates, and that too many vitamins can be as dangerous as too few. Also, fat-soluble vitamins are stored in the body, so excessive quantities may eventually produce toxic effects.

VITAMINS AND/OR MINERALS SHOULD NOT BE GIVEN WITHOUT FIRST CONSULTING YOUR DOCTOR.

The fat-soluble vitamins are A, D, E, and K, and the water-soluble vitamins are the B complex group and C. Fat-soluble vitamins can be stored by the body for later use, but unused water-soluble vitamins are excreted in the urine. Foods containing the water-soluble vitamins must be eaten daily in order to supply the body constantly.

VITAMIN A helps keep the skin healthy and protects it from becoming rough and dry. An insufficiency of this vitamin can cause nails to split or become ridged, and hair will lose its luster and grow dry and brittle. It is important for growth, strong bones, and healthy teeth in children. The linings of the gastrointestinal and respiratory tracts require vitamin A to function properly. It also helps build resistance to infection. Vitamin A is necessary for good vision and protects against night blindness.

Symptoms of vitamin A deficiency are night blindness, stunted growth, tooth and gum decay, loss of appetite, dry or scaly skin, loss of vigor, sinus trouble, and increased susceptibility to infection. However, vitamin A deficiency is rare in this country, and toxicity caused by taking excessive amounts does occur.

Best food sources for vitamin A are liver, fish liver oils, butter, milk, and egg yolk.

Beta carotene is a provitamin from which the body manufactures vitamin A. Extensive research is being conducted on the effect of beta carotene in preventing lung cancer and possibly other cancers. Beta carotene cannot be taken in vitamin A pills, but must be ingested through fruits and vegetables containing this substance.

Sources rich in carotene are sweet potatoes, carrots, collard greens, beet greens, spinach, pumpkin, butternut squash, tomatoes, broccoli, red peppers, winter squash, cantaloupe, apricots, papayas, peaches, and nectarines.

The vitamin B complex group contains eight water-soluble vitamins: B_1 (thiamine), B_2 (riboflavin), B_6 (pyridoxine), B_{12} (cyanocobalamin), niacin, folic acid, pantothenic acid, and biotin.

VITAMIN B_1 (thiamine) is necessary for growth, good appetite and digestion, and healthy nerves. It helps the body release food-supplied energy.

Best food sources are pork, organ meats, whole grains, brewers' yeast, eggs, and cereals.

VITAMIN B_2 (riboflavin) helps blood cells utilize oxygen. It also assists in maintaining good vision and is needed in certain enzymes that help change food into energy. Important for smooth skin, it is beneficial in preventing scaling or cracking of skin around the mouth and nose.

Good sources are liver, milk and milk products, green leafy vegetables, meats, eggs, whole-grain and enriched bread, cereals.

VITAMIN B_6 (pyridoxine) is necessary for growth and a healthy nervous system.

Best food sources are organ meats, pork, bran, and wheat germ.

VITAMIN B_{12} (cyanocobalamin) is involved in many processes necessary to metabolize proteins, fats, and carbohydrates. It also participates in the formation of red blood cells. Deficiency of this vitamin is uncommon except in children who have been put on a vegan diet (no animal protein, milk, eggs, or cheese).

Symptoms of deficiency include tiredness, breathlessness, sore tongue, nervous lesions, and megaloblastic anemia. Serious deficiency may cause irreversible neurological damage unless diagnosed and treated early.

Vitamin B_{12} occurs only in animal foods. Lean meats, liver, kidney, eggs, and fish are all excellent sources. Vitamin B_{12} is also found in milk and cheese.

NIACIN promotes normal appetite and digestion and is necessary for a healthy nervous system. It is also needed in certain enzymes that help convert food into energy.

Good sources of niacin are liver, meats, fish, poultry, green vegetables, nuts (especially peanuts), whole-grain breads and cereals (except corn), and enriched breads and cereals.

FOLIC ACID (folacin) is important for proper development of red blood cells.

Best food sources are green leafy vegetables, liver, beef, yeast, and orange juice.

PANTOTHENIC ACID aids in metabolism and the synthesis of adrenal hormones.

Best food sources are eggs, liver, and salmon. However, all animal and plant foods contain certain amounts of pantothenic acid.

BIOTIN assists in metabolism of proteins, carbohydrates, and fats.
Best food sources are liver, peanuts, milk, meats, most vegetables, egg yolk, brewers' yeast, and brown rice.

VITAMIN C (ascorbic acid) has many functions. It helps gastrointestinal absorption of iron and calcium, protects vitamin A and E, and is necessary for formation of certain substances that cement bone cells, teeth, connective tissue, and capillaries. Vitamin C provides resistance to disease and aids in healing wounds.

VITAMIN TABLE*						
Water-Soluble Vitamins						
Vit. B_1 (mg)	Vit. B_2 (mg)	Vit. B_6 (mg)	Vit. B_{12} (μg)	Nia- cin (mg)	Folic Acid (μg)	Vit. C (mg)
Infants 0.5–1 yr. 0.5	0.6	0.6	1.5	8	45	35
Children 1–3 yrs. 0.7	0.8	0.9	2.0	9	100	45

Legend: g = gram   1 g = .035 ounce   1 ounce = 28.35 g.
mg = milligram, one thousandth of a gram
μg = microgram, one millionth of a gram

Fat-Soluble Vitamins		
Vit. A (IU)	Vit. D (IU)	Vit. E (IU)
Infants 0.5–1 yr. 2,000	400	4
Children 1–3 yrs. 2,000	400	5

Note: IU = International Units
*Source: *Recommended Dietary Allowances*, Revised 1980, Food and Nutrition Board, National Academy of Sciences, National Research Council, Washington, D.C.

Vitamin C should be replenished daily. It is lost rapidly when kept at room temperature, but much less so when refrigerated. Frozen foods should not be thawed before cooking, as this causes a great loss of vitamin C. Vegetables should be either steamed or cooked in a tightly covered pan with a small amount of liquid, over a low heat. Soda should never be used in cooking vegetables, as it destroys vitamin C.

Vitamin C deficiency causes scurvy (symptoms are tender, painful muscles, joints, and bones, muscle cramps, and loss of appetite) and gum disease.

Best vegetable sources are broccoli, Brussels sprouts, cabbage, cauliflower, spinach, red and green peppers, tomatoes, and potatoes.

Best fruit sources for vitamin C are cantaloupe, grapefruit, oranges, limes, lemons, strawberries, tangerines, kiwi fruit, and watermelon.

VITAMIN D is important in building strong bones and teeth. A daily supply is necessary for the body to use calcium from food and to release calcium stored in the bones. Some vitamin D can be produced by the body through the action of direct sunlight on the skin. If sunshine is not available, a dietary source of vitamin D is essential.

Best food source is fish liver oils. However, these are seldom included in most diets because of the taste, and children refuse them. Other sources are vitamin D fortified milk, egg yolk, and liver.

VITAMIN E prevents destruction of certain other nutrients (vitamin A) in the body and aids in the proper use of energy supplied by glucose and fatty acids. It is also necessary for healthy red blood cells.

This vitamin is found primarily in foods of plant origin, such as vegetable oils, wheat germ, nuts, whole-grain breads and cereals, and dark green leafy vegetables.

VITAMIN K is necessary for normal clotting of blood. Dietary requirements for this vitamin are normally quite low because it is formed in the intestine.

Vitamin K sources are found in a variety of vegetables such as cabbage, cauliflower, spinach, Swiss chard, and beet tops.

MINERALS

Minerals are needed for our health and well-being. They have two general functions, to build and regulate the body. Each mineral has a special activity which is of equal importance to the others. The building function affects the skeleton and all soft tissue, and the regulation function involves a wide variety of systems such as heartbeat, blood clotting, maintenance of the internal pressure of body fluids, nerve responses, and transportation of oxygen from the lungs to the tissues.

Some of these functions require large quantities of minerals, while others may only need minute traces. Without minerals, the vitamins cannot perfect their work. However, minerals can be harmful if taken in excess, and each year many children under five years of age are hospitalized with iron poisoning caused by accidentally swallowing multiple vitamin and mineral supplements. A balanced diet usually supplies all the minerals the body needs.

In cooking vegetables and grains, it is essential that excessive heat be avoided, that a minimum of water be used, and that airtight lids cover saucepans to prevent oxidation in order to retain maximum nutrients and avoid loss of precious minerals.

Minerals found in the human body fall into two groups: *major minerals*, if present in large amounts; and *trace minerals*, if present in small amounts and with a known function, or if present in small amounts with a function that is not understood.

Major minerals are calcium, phosphorus, magnesium, sodium, potassium, chlorine, and sulfur.

Trace minerals with known functions are iron, copper, iodine, manganese, cobalt, zinc, and molybdenum. Trace minerals with functions that are not understood are fluoride, selenium, aluminum, boron, cadmium, chromium, nickel, tin, silicon, and vanadium.

Of all the minerals listed above, calcium, potassium, phosphorus, magnesium, copper, zinc, fluoride, iodine, and iron will be dealt with here in more detail.

CALCIUM is the mineral found in the body in the largest quantity. It is essential for the formation of strong bones and teeth. Although 99 percent of the body's calcium is in the bones and teeth, the remaining 1 percent is in the blood, body fluids, and soft tissues, where it plays a very important role.

Calcium is required for proper blood clotting, transmission of nerve impulses, and contraction and relaxation of the heart. These

CALCIUM CONTENT OF SOME COMMON FOODS		
Food	*Amount*	*Calcium (mg)*
Plain yogurt	1 cup	425
Fruit and flavored yogurt	1 cup	380
Sardines with bones	3 oz.	360
Milk (whole, low fat, nonfat, buttermilk, chocolate)	1 cup	300
Swiss and Gruyère cheeses	1 oz.	270
Hard cheeses (cheddar, Monterey jack, Edam, Muenster)	1 oz.	200
Processed cheeses	1 oz.	175
Salmon with bones	3 oz.	170
Collard greens	½ cup	170
Cheese spreads	1 oz.	160
Soft cheeses (mozzarella, blue, feta)	1 oz.	150
Cheese foods	1 oz.	140
Turnip greens, kale, dandelion greens	½ cup	100
Cooked dried beans (navy, pea, and lima)	1 cup	90

functions are so important that the body will extract calcium from the bones if necessary.

Growing children need large amounts of calcium. The daily requirement for infants six months to one year is 540 milligrams for children one to three years, it is 800 milligrams daily. A healthy person normally absorbs 20 percent to 30 percent of the calcium ingested. As and if the need for calcium increases, so does its absorption by the body, and growing children may absorb up to 75 percent of the calcium they consume.

Calcium absorption is promoted by the presence of lactose, vitamin D, and the parathyroid hormone, while a dietary excess of phosphorus will hinder calcium absorption. Many commercial soft drinks, and especially colas, contain phosphoric acid.

The best food sources of calcium are milk and dairy products, sardines and salmon with bones, dark green leafy vegetables (except spinach), and dried beans.

POTASSIUM acts in balance with sodium as a major control for water distribution in the body. It is about twice as plentiful in the body as sodium. The average diet contains an ample supply of potassium, so a deficiency is unlikely. This mineral is widely distributed in natural foods such as legumes, whole grains, green leafy vegetables, and meats, and in certain fruits like bananas, dates, oranges, and dried prunes.

PHOSPHORUS. Eighty percent of the body's phosphorus is found in the bones. The remaining 20 percent is contained in muscle and blood serum. Phosphorus is a necessary constituent of every cell in the body.

Recommended intakes of phosphorus are the same as for calcium, except during infancy when a dietary calcium-to-phosphorus ratio of 1.5 to 1 is recommended. Phosphorus is found along with calcium in dairy products, but it also exists in foods containing little calcium, including such protein-rich foods as meats, eggs, nuts, and legumes. It is also found in grains and is present in many carbonated beverages.

MAGNESIUM is the fourth most abundant mineral in the body; approximately 50 percent of it is found in the bones, along with calcium and phosphorus, 25 percent in the muscles, and the remainder in soft tissue. It is necessary for the production and transfer of energy and helps conduct the nerve impulses that relax muscles following contraction. Magnesium also seems to promote calcium retention in tooth enamel and increase resistance to dental cavities.

Magnesium is relatively widespread in nature. Nuts, whole grains, soybeans, legumes, and shellfish are excellent sources. It exists in all green plants as a component of chlorophyll. Cow's milk contains 12 milligrams to 100 milliliters of magnesium.

COPPER. Trace amounts of copper are distributed in all tissues throughout the body. The highest concentration of this mineral is found in the liver, brain, and kidneys. One of copper's most important functions is to facilitate the absorption and transportation of iron throughout the body.

The requirement for copper is so low, and it appears in so many foods, that deficiencies are unlikely to occur in normal children who consume a variety of foods.

The richest sources of copper are shellfish, organ meats, dried legumes, eggs, and nuts. Substantial quantities of copper may be present in drinking water supplied through copper pipes, especially in soft-water areas.

ZINC. The biological role of zinc has been recognized for more than a hundred years, but only recently has its importance attracted attention in nutrition. The human body contains only about 2 grams of zinc, yet this mineral is absolutely essential for proper growth and development and for normal body functioning.

Zinc plays diverse roles in everyday life. It is vital for the health of the skin, the healing of wounds, and maintaining a normal sense of taste. It is a component of many enzymes involved in metabolism, and it is essential for the formation of the nucleic acids RNA and DNA, the basic materials of genes. Zinc enhances the action of a number of hormones, including insulin, and is essential for normal growth and development of the embryo and newborn infant. The possibility of zinc deficiency should be considered in any child with poor appetite and slow growth. Recommended dietary allowance of zinc for children six months to one year is 5 milligrams and for children one to three years of age, 10 milligrams.

Zinc-rich foods include organ meats (2 ounces of liver contain about 4 milligrams of zinc), muscle meats (the dark meat of poultry is a particularly good source, with 3 ounces providing 2.4 milligrams), dairy products (a cup of milk contains 1 milligram), and eggs (one egg contains 0.5 milligram). Whole-grain cereals are high in zinc, but they also contain substances called phytates that combine with the mineral and interfere with absorption. However, when whole grains are sprouted or used in making bread with yeast, the phytates are inactivated, allowing for more efficient absorption. Like most trace minerals, much of the zinc is removed when grains are processed, so breads and cereals made from refined flours are gen-

ZINC CONTENT OF SOME COMMON FOODS		
Food	*Amount*	*Zinc (mg)*
Cow's milk	4 oz.	0.5
Ground beef, cooked	2 oz.	2.5
Chicken drumstick	1	1.4
Beef liver, cooked	2 oz.	2.9
Liverwurst	1 oz.	0.8
Frankfurter	1	0.9
Egg	1 medium	0.5
Oatmeal, cooked	½ cup	0.6
Bread, whole wheat	1 slice	0.5
Bread, white	1 slice	0.2
Spinach	½ cup	0.6
Banana	½ medium	0.2
Orange, small	1	0.3

erally a poor source. The key to getting enough zinc is to have a diet containing plenty of fresh and minimally processed foods, in addition to the high-zinc food sources.

FLUORIDE in the body is concentrated in the bones and teeth. It is present in soft tissue and body fluids only in minute quantities. The known role of this essential trace mineral is its ability to reduce dental cavities. All foods contain very small amounts of fluoride, with the exception of certain seafoods.

Public health authorities advocate fluoridation of public drinking water that is low in fluoride content. Many doctors recommend supplementing the diets of infants and children up to the age of sixteen, with dosages adjusted to the concentration of fluoride in the drinking water. This is still a very controversial issue, and each family should discuss it with a pediatrician before deciding on fluoride supplementation.

IODINE. The largest amount of iodine in the body is focused in the thyroid gland, and small amounts are present in the blood, skin, and other tissues. The thyroid hormones regulate energy metabolism. The conversion of carotene to vitamin A, the synthesis of proteins, and the intestinal absorption of carbohydrates are more efficient when thyroid hormone levels are normal.

The recommended daily requirement for iodine has recently been increased. For infants six months to one year, it is 50 micrograms (a microgram is one millionth of a gram), and for children one to three, it is 70 micrograms.

Iodized salt, milk, and seafood are the best sources of dietary iodine. The fact that the iodine content of food is determined by the soil in which the food is grown is no longer significant in the etiology of iodine deficiency. Food that is consumed in one area is often transported from another. It has also become a practice to enrich animal feeds with iodine in places where the soil is deficient in it.

IRON is the most abundant trace mineral in the body. It is necessary for the formation of hemoglobin, which carries oxygen to the body's cells and carbon dioxide away from the tissues. The recom-

IRON CONTENT OF SOME COMMON FOODS		
Food	Amount	Iron (mg)
Iron-fortified formula	8 oz.	3.0
Infant cereal, high protein	1 tbsp.	1.1
Infant cereal, rice	1 tbsp.	1.1
Strained beef with vegetables	1 oz.	0.3
Strained split peas with ham	1 oz.	0.2
Strained vegetables and chicken	1 oz.	0.1
Strained beef	1 oz.	0.6
Strained liver	1 oz.	1.6
Hamburger, cooked	2 oz.	1.8
Chicken, dark meat	1 oz.	0.5
Beef liver	1 oz.	2.5
Chicken liver	1 liver	2.1
Liverwurst	1 oz.	1.7
Frankfurter	1	0.9
Egg	1 medium	1.0
Pork and beans	¼ cup	1.5
Peanut butter	1 tbsp.	0.3
Bread, enriched white	1 slice	0.7
Macaroni, enriched, cooked	¼ cup	0.4
Carrots, cooked	¼ cup	0.2
Orange	1 medium	0.6
Canned pears	¼ cup	0.1

MINERAL TABLE*					
Calcium (mg)	Phosphorus (mg)	Magnesium (mg)	Zinc (mg)	Iodine (μg)	Iron (mg)
Infants					
0.5–1 yr. 540	360	70	5	50	15
Children					
1–3 yrs. 800	800	150	10	70	15

Legend: μg = microgram (one millionth of a gram)

mg = milligram (one thousandth of a gram)

g = gram

*Source: *Recommended Dietary Allowances*, Revised 1980, Food and Nutrition Board, National Academy of Sciences, National Research Council, Washington, D.C.

mended daily allowance for children six months to three years is 15 milligrams.

In a medically sophisticated and wealthy country like the United States, it is surprising that nearly 30 percent of children between six months and thirty months from lower-socioeconomic backgrounds and 5 percent of children from upper-middle-class families suffer from iron deficiency anemia.

Four factors determine adequate iron supplies in infants and children:

· Iron endowment at birth
· Relative growth rate
· Occult-blood loss
· Iron intake and absorption

The best indication of iron endowment at birth is birth weight. Occult-blood loss is found in the stools (bowel movements). It is usually associated with the ingestion of large amounts (one to two quarts) of fresh whole homogenized milk before the child is six months of age.

Although there may be a large intake of iron, intestinal absorption may vary. Different types of iron also affect absorption. Only approximately 10 percent of the iron taken in by infants and children is absorbed.

Once an infant starts on solids, the best source of iron is iron-fortified baby cereal. Few commercially prepared baby foods provide generous amounts of iron, with the exception of pure beef and liver. Organ meats, dried legumes, shellfish, and muscle meats provide the richest and most usable sources of iron. Other sources include nuts, green leafy vegetables, and whole wheat flour and bread.

Feeding Children

FEEDING children well can be a challenge to any parent. In many homes, a child's eating habits and mealtime behavior are a source of great stress for both parents and child. Parents who adopt a relaxed attitude toward food and mealtimes are more successful in getting their children to eat nutritious, well-balanced meals. However, any child's appetite can fluctuate from month to month, especially while he goes through the teething process for the first two years or so.

Mealtimes should be and can be enjoyable for parents and baby, although it may occasionally take a conscious effort to make them so. There is no way of getting around the fact that a baby learning to eat solid foods creates a mess. After every meal during this stage, the child, high chair, floor, and often parent have to be washed. If you can remember that this stage doesn't last forever and learn to be prepared, it can be fun.

It is to every child's advantage to be exposed to a wide variety of foods, although they do not need highly seasoned foods. It is fine to introduce Mexican, Indian, or other ethnic dishes with various herbs and spices, but the flavors should be mild. Children prefer the natural taste of foods, and salt can be eliminated in most cooking.

What a child eats is much more important than how much he eats. Parental buying habits can do much to diminish the problems of bad eating habits. If nonnutritive foods are not in your home in the first place, they cannot be consumed by the child. If a child is not exposed to cookies, candies, and other sweets, he is not going to insist on them in place of vegetables, fruit, cheese, or meat.

Parents may not be aware of how little food a child needs, especially when he is switched from baby to table food. Infants cannot eat and do not need adult-size portions. The age at which many children begin eating table food (twelve months to two years) coincides with the age at which the growth rate and appetite of children naturally decrease. As a guideline: *The average child can be expected to eat one tablespoonful of each type of food at each meal for each year of his age.*

From about one and a half years on, the child starts to be demanding and fussy and can be adamant about what he wants and doesn't want. Coaxing or persuasion seldom helps. That is why establishing the child's taste for nutritious, wholesome foods from the very beginning is so important. His tastes are going to change, and some of the foods he accepted earlier are likely to be flatly refused now. But a child's basic food preferences are going to remain unless parents unknowingly change them.

Children are usually notoriously reluctant to eat vegetables. It seems to me that the way they are served and how frequently, have a lot to do with this reaction. Vegetables served freshly steamed look and taste so much better than puréed spinach or peas and carrots from a jar. Homemade soups made with a milk base, fresh vegetables, and small pieces of meat and/or rice and beans can ensure that a baby gets his vegetables, even a complete meal, that can be taken from a cup.

Children usually enjoy fruits, so offer them for desserts instead of cookies, cakes, and Jell-O. Dried fruits are wonderful finger foods, and are readily accepted by children in place of candy. Dried pitted dates, prunes, and apricots are also good sources of vitamins and minerals.

Don't fill up your child with snacks such as potato chips, cookies, and crackers. If an hour or two after eating a substantial meal he appears hungry, offer fruit, cheese, vegetables, yogurt; or a piece of whole wheat bread, a cup of milk, or a fruit or milk drink.

Be sensitive to your little one's own signs telling you what he wants and how he feels, and don't project your desires, decisions, or fears onto your baby. Feed him only when he is hungry. Be relaxed and unconcerned if he refuses food for one or two meals. Here we are talking about healthy babies. However, if you suspect that your child may be sick, you should consult a physician.

Lastly, let your baby feed himself as soon as he is able, regardless of the mess. Make the atmosphere happy, with smiles, laughter, music if you like, and love.

MILK

Because of its high nutritional value, milk is important to our diet. According to the U.S. Department of Agriculture, dairy products (excluding butter) contribute only 11 percent of food energy (calories), but provide 75 percent of the calcium, 39 percent of the riboflavin, 35 percent of the phosphorus, 22 percent of the magnesium, 20 percent of the vitamin B_{12}, and substantial quantities of other nutrients necessary to a healthful diet.

In its latest study (August 1983), the American Academy of Pediatrics has recommended that infants not be given whole cow's milk prior to six months of age, but be either breast-fed or receive iron-fortified formulas. Pasteurized whole milk can be given from six months on, provided that the infant receives supplemental iron through iron-fortified cereal or is consuming one third of his calories through a balanced mixture of cereal, vegetables, fruits, and other foods, thereby ensuring adequate amounts of iron and vitamin C. If large amounts of whole milk (one quart or more per day) are consumed without the benefit of supplemental iron, serious iron deficiencies may occur. As milk is low in iron, such large quantities would replace the iron-rich foods that should be part of a whole-milk diet.

With the current emphasis on diets lower in fat and cholesterol, mothers may feel inclined to give their infants or toddlers skim or low-fat milk. Fat-reduced milk should not be given to children under two years of age, as it will deprive them of necessary calories and reduce their intake of fats and fatty acids. Diets of normal infants and toddlers should not be restricted this way.

Many Hispanics, Native Americans, Orientals, and blacks have high incidences of lactose intolerance, a condition in which there is an inability to digest lactose (milk sugar) because of a deficiency of the enzyme lactase. Some symptoms of this condition may be diarrhea, flatulence (gas), abdominal cramps, and bloating. However, the use of milk and milk products should not be discouraged completely, as lactose intolerance to as much as a cup of milk consumed at one time is rare in preadolescents. (Additional sources of calcium are sardines, salmon with bones, turnip greens, and cooked dried beans, among others, but a toddler would not receive an adequate supply from these sources because he would have to eat such large quantities to do so.)

As well as being a good source of protein, calcium, and other valuable nutrients, milk also is sold fortified with vitamin D. The lactose and vitamin D in milk aid in calcium absorption.

There is still some dispute as to the benefits of raw (certified) milk versus pasteurized milk. Raw milk may be more palatable and nutritionally superior, but the American Academy of Pediatrics' Committee on Infectious Diseases believes that, on balance, the risk of serious disease outweighs the potential benefits of the widespread use of raw milk, and it endorses pasteurized milk whenever whole milk is prescribed for infants and children.

SALT

Sodium, a component of salt or sodium chloride, is one of the more plentiful major minerals in the body and is critical to many metabolic activities. It controls the volume of body fluids and water balance, helps relax contracted muscles (in the presence of potassium), facilitates the absorption of various nutrients, including glucose, and transmits nerve impulses.

Throughout the ages, salt has been considered a precious mineral, and used as one of the world's principal trading commodities. During the late eighteenth century, the rank of guests at a banquet was gauged by where they sat in relation to an elaborate silver saltcellar on the table. The host and distinguished guests sat at the head of the table, above the salt. Those who sat below the salt, farthest from the host, were of little consequence. Today, almost two hundred years later, that etiquette could work in reverse.

What has caused a mineral that was once so valued to become our dietary Enemy Number One? Basically most foods contain some sodium, including our drinking water. Salt is used in cooking, then it is added again at the table. We now have an abundance of salt and use a great deal more than we need, feeling that our meals taste bland without it.

Salt, of course, is a taste that one becomes accustomed to. Babies are born with pure "taste buds" and no bad eating habits, and these can be avoided if they are given unadulterated foods. Eating patterns are formed early that will stay with a child for the rest of his life.

Statistically it has been shown that there are excessive incidences of hypertension (high blood pressure) in countries where there is a high intake of salt, and hypertension is one of the major health problems of North America. Both hereditary and environmental factors are involved. Studies have shown that children are at greater risk when there is a family history of hypertension. Among environmental factors, salt in the diet has been cited as a possible contributing element. Although there is no definite proof that some humans are particularly sensitive to high salt intake, animal studies have raised that speculation. With individuals potentially at risk, a high salt intake at infancy might predispose them to developing hypertension in later life.

In a long-term survey of infant nutrition, published in the *Journal of the American Dietetic Association* (March 1982), it was suggested that salt should not be added to homemade baby foods, nor should infants be given canned products containing added salt. The study revealed that milk and milk products alone provide enough sodium to meet the recommended salt intake level for children up to eighteen months of age. It was also found that sodium intake from homemade foods was relatively low during the first six months of life, with a marked increase from six to eight months, and a sharp increase from eight months onward. This was attributed to the use of table foods, which were introduced at the average age of seven months. Eleven percent or less of a baby's total sodium intake before six months was contributed by home-prepared foods. A rapid increase to 52 percent, 60 percent, 72 percent, and 77 percent was noted at ten, twelve, fifteen, and eighteen months of age, respectively.

To give some indication of how much salt is present in certain foods, corn has only 1 milligram; cornflakes have 256 milligrams per cup; a potato has 5 milligrams; ten potato chips have 200 milligrams; a frozen meat-loaf dinner has 1,305 milligrams; a cup of tomato soup has 932 milligrams; and a fast-food chicken dinner contains 2,243 milligrams of salt. The estimated safe and adequate daily dietary allowance of sodium for a six- to twelve-month-old is 250 to 750 milligrams. From one to three years of age, the suggested intake is 325 to 973 milligrams per day.*

(The relationship between sodium and salt may be confusing. Salt is composed of two elements, sodium and chloride. Each molecule of salt is 40 percent sodium. One level teaspoon of salt weighing 7 grams contains 2.8 grams, or 2,800 milligrams of sodium.)

I have always been very conscious of adding little or no salt or sugar to my baby's food, and never use salt when boiling potatoes, macaroni, vegetables, or spaghetti. Occasionally I add a little salt to a recipe, but prefer to add other herbs, spices, and flavors to enhance the food. I feel all of this is beneficial to my whole family's well-being. Although I have not specified it in all applicable recipes, I believe it is wise and preferable to use unsalted (sweet) butter.

---

*1,000 milligrams = 1 gram

SUGAR

The subject of sugar is as controversial as that of salt. Sugar has virtually no nutritional value, destroys the appetite, promotes tooth decay, and is otherwise known as "empty calories." As with salt, most foods contain some form of sugar.

The food industry uses sugar liberally as a preservative as well as to sweeten such foods as cakes, cookies, and cereals, some of which are more than 50 percent sugar! Many foods that do not appear to be sweet, such as catsup, bread, canned corn, and mustard, also contain sugar. To avoid an excess of sugar in the diet, it is important to read food labels when shopping, remembering that ingredients are listed in order of quantity.

Some people feel that turbinado sugar, which is partially refined, is more nutritious than white sugar. However, studies by Krehl and Cowgill at Yale University School of Medicine concluded that raw sugar and other sugar products, including brown sugar, contain such small quantities of vitamins as to be insignificant. However, the darkest brown sugar available does contain small amounts of calcium, phosphorus, iron, sodium, and potassium. Blackstrap molasses, perhaps the most "beneficial" of the sweeteners, contains the B-complex vitamins, iron, calcium, copper, magnesium, potassium, and phosphorus as well as being 50 percent natural sugar.

Honey is easily assimilated and is therefore more digestible, but should not be given to babies, as it may contain botulism spores.

Chocolate is another controversial sweet that contains empty calories and promotes tooth decay. It also contains caffeine, theobromine, and oxalic acid, which are not recommended for babies. Carob—high in iron, minerals, calcium, and vitamins, and low in fat—can be substituted for chocolate. However, it is suggested that all sweets and sweeteners be given extremely sparingly to young children to prevent the encouragement of a sweet tooth.

NURSING BOTTLE SYNDROME
AND YOUR BABY'S TEETH

Bottle feeding is one method of giving an infant nourishment, but too often the nursing bottle, containing juice, is misused as a pacifier to comfort or control infant behavior.

As soon as an infant has teeth, he is susceptible to tooth decay. The strength and health of his teeth may well depend on bottle feeding habits that are established as soon as he starts taking juices. If a child is given juice from a bottle, the sugar-rich liquid gathers in pools around his upper teeth; this can eventually cause tooth decay. Nursing bottle cavities destroy practically all the upper deciduous (baby) teeth because of prolonged contact with juices fed by bottle. The cavities are painful and unattractive, and the teeth may break or become impossible to repair. If primary teeth are lost too early in life, the incoming permanent teeth may be crowded or crooked. The decay or early loss of primary teeth could also cause speech problems later on as well as a poor self-image and loss of appetite (as cold, hot, or hard foods may be difficult or painful to eat). The loss of appetite may eliminate food that is important to a well-balanced diet.

The following points should be kept in mind in preventing nursing bottle syndrome:

- Start infants on juice from a cup; never give it from a bottle.
- Do not put your child to bed at night with a bottle. Even milk and formulas containing many nutrients vital to the development of teeth should not be used as a pacifier at nap or bedtime. (Milk does not normally promote decay, but it too can become harmful if allowed to remain in the mouth for long periods.) If your child

must have a bottle at naptime, between feedings, at night, or for comfort, give only fresh water.
- Never use a pacifier dipped in honey or other sweeteners.
- Clean the infant's or toddler's teeth properly. Wipe teeth and gums after each feeding with a damp washcloth or a gauze pad to remove plaque. Continue this practice until all primary teeth have erupted (at about two or two and one half years of age), or until the child is old enough to brush, then use a child's toothbrush with short, rounded bristles (and later also use dental floss).
- A well-balanced diet is important to sustain healthy teeth and gum tissue. Serve food from each of the four food groups at every meal—milk, protein/meat, vegetable/fruit, bread/cereal.
- Limit foods containing sugar. If you do offer candy, cookies, or other sweets, give them only occasionally at mealtimes, not as snacks. This will limit the number of times the teeth are exposed to the acid that leads to decay.
- Serve a food at the end of each meal that will help clear the mouth of food particles, increase salivary flow, and act as a buffer to neutralize the acid that destroys teeth. Swiss, Monterey Jack, or cheddar cheeses, as well as raw apples, carrots, and celery, are all good choices.
- Start the habit of visiting the dentist for regular checkups at around the child's second birthday.
- Keep in mind the use of fluoridated drinking water has been found to help prevent cavities.

The following is a statement recently released by the American Academy of Pediatrics and the American Academy of Pedodontists:

The use of juices from a bottle should be discouraged; infants should be offered juice from a cup as soon as possible. Nursing bottle caries can be avoided if milk in a bottle is not used as a pacifier at nap or bedtime, if milk bottle feeding is discontinued soon after the first birthday, and if juice is always offered from a cup.

CHILDHOOD OBESITY

A chubby baby is usually considered to be cute, happy, and healthy. Whether or not there is any truth to this notion, one serious question still remains: Does a fat baby become a fat adult?

Although research in this area has been limited until recently, and even now is far from complete, current medical opinion seems to support this dismal prognosis. Obesity appears to be caused more by overeating, particularly excessive quantities of fats and refined carbohydrates, than by heredity. If a child develops poor eating habits early in life, he tends to continue them in later years. Recent medical evidence has revealed that an overweight infant may have twice as many fat cells as an infant of normal weight of the same age. Once fat cells have developed, they do not decrease, and their numbers influence the amount of fat that is ultimately stored in the body. An overweight child will tend to be an overweight adult.

Considering the physical and psychological suffering that accompanies obesity, as well as the time and money spent on weight reduction in this country, the importance of the above findings cannot be overemphasized.

Good eating habits and a nutritious diet will go a long way toward reducing the possibility of your child suffering from weight problems later in life.

Here are some preventive measures worth adopting for your baby:

· Don't sweeten cereals. If you don't start using sugar on cereals, your baby will get used to the basic taste and will not demand sweeteners.
· If your baby will not accept cereals, try adding fresh fruit such as bananas, apples, pears, peaches, or prunes. These will also provide important vitamins and minerals.

· Don't insist on your child eating every last spoonful. You don't know the extent of his appetite for that meal, so watch carefully for the first sign that he has had enough.

· Don't get angry or upset when your baby's attention is distracted, when food is spat out, rubbed in the hair or high chair, and his mouth clamps shut. You are being told, "Enough, thank you," and it is important for you to listen to the message. Quietly remove all food, or mealtimes may become a battleground for attention as well as a test of wills, which is the last thing you want.

· If your child is hurt or unhappy, don't comfort him with food or candy. Give him love, hugs, and kisses. One of the hardest habits to avoid is giving your baby a bottle to quiet him down. But if you don't start the habit, you won't have to break it.

· Don't be fanatical about never allowing your little one to have cakes, cookies, or candies. A good rule is to allow sweets on special occasions such as holidays and birthdays. They should not be allowed on a daily basis. If your infant has not been totally deprived of sweets, he is not likely to rebel and go to the other extreme as an adult. (An added bonus to this rule is that treats given only occasionally seem to give even greater pleasure as something very special.)

· Turkey, chicken, veal, and liver are poultry and meats most recommended for babies. Serve beef, lamb, pork, and ham less frequently. Choose lean ground and other cuts of meat. Trim all visible fat before cooking. Use the following meats very sparingly: mutton, spareribs, frankfurters, sausages, fatty hamburgers, bacon, luncheon meat, and heavily marbled meats.

· Bake, broil, or steam food rather than fry it.

· Avoid frequent use of gravies and sauces made with butter, fats, or cream. Don't use commercial coating mixes, as they contain large amounts of sugar and fat.

· Children love pasta and bread and usually choose them over vegetables. Be careful not to feed your child excessive amounts of starches to the exclusion of other basic foods.

ALLERGIES

Food allergies are very common among infants, toddlers, and children, but are sometimes very difficult to diagnose. A doctor should always be consulted to correctly identify any allergy, as a wrong diagnosis could eliminate important staple foods from the diet, thereby preventing the child from receiving optimal nutrition.

Before starting a baby on solids, the parents should check both sides of the family to ascertain if there are tendencies toward allergies to specific foods. If so, those foods should be avoided until after the child is one year of age.

Many infants show intolerance toward certain foods either because their digestive systems are insufficiently developed or because of allergic reactions to certain foods. When introducing a new food into an infant's diet, watch carefully for any negative reaction, such as diarrhea, vomiting, fever, rash, swelling, or itching. Always wait at least four days before introducing another new food so that the problem food can be easily identified if a reaction should occur.

The following list shows foods commonly known to cause allergies

Possible Allergy/Intolerance Food	May be offered at . . .
Milk, milk products (i.e., cheese, yogurt, etc.), egg yolk	Six months
Wheat, buckwheat, semolina, citrus fruits and juices, cooked tomatoes	Eight months
Fish, shellfish, egg whites, peanuts* and other nuts,* corn, berries, raw tomatoes, cocoa, chocolate	Latter part of the first year

*Note: As nuts are potential choke foods, they should be introduced to the infant in the form of nut butters.

or intolerance in babies, and the suggested time to introduce them
into the diet. If any reaction is noted, discontinue feeding *immediately* and consult a doctor.

INTRODUCING SOLIDS

Fifty years ago the most common age to introduce solid foods to
babies was at twelve months. Twenty years ago, when my first child
was born, the pediatrician suggested starting solids and juices at
six weeks. Today, the consensus is that six months is the right time.
At this age, most of an infant's supply of iron has been used up
and, since neither human nor cow's milk contains an adequate amount
of iron an infant who is fed only milk may develop anemia.

Until a baby is six months of age, the enzymes in his system are
equipped only to digest mother's milk or a reasonably close substitute. At six months, however, the necessary enzymes are developed
so a baby can digest solid food.

Solids given too early may lessen a baby's appetite for milk or
formula and rob him of essential nutrients. According to the American Academy of Pediatrics, children who are fed semisolids prior
to four to six months of age are not advanced nutritionally or developmentally and, in fact, may be hindered because of their reduced
intake of milk. Many doctors and nutritionists also feel that food
introduced earlier than six months may cause allergic reactions in
sensitive children and tend to cause obesity later in life.

There are differences of opinion whether to feed solids before
nursing or bottle feeding, or afterward. One theory suggests introducing solid food when your baby is hungry and will be more eager
to accept it; another is that if the baby is really hungry and waiting
for the breast or bottle, but is offered a spoon with strange-tasting
stuff on it, he will be furious and want no part of it. Choose the
method you feel is best. Tune in to your little one and listen, feel,
and observe all he is telling you, even though he cannot talk. Re-

member, you know your baby better than anyone else.

Be patient and understanding. Until now, sucking has been all your child has needed to satisfy his hunger. Suddenly he has to figure out how to get this unusually flavored and textured mixture off a spoon and into his mouth. No easy task, and some of the food will cover a much wider territory than his mouth for a while. If you can look at these first attempts at feeding as fun and not be nervous, it will be an adventure. You will also both improve with practice.

Use a slim shallow spoon and always try to put the spoon *on* your baby's tongue. Start with small servings (about ½ tablespoonful) and take your time. However, don't spend more than twenty to thirty minutes on each meal. Relax and enjoy, as the mood you establish at this point is as important as the food you are teaching your child to eat.

If some food needs thinning down, and your infant cannot or will not tolerate pasteurized cow's milk, use your breast milk. Alternatively, you can give him goat milk or soy milk products, which are easily digested. Keep all cooked food temperatures between tepid and warm. Test each dish yourself first, as hot food is frightening and may burn your baby's mouth.

What should baby's first meal consist of?

Talk to your pediatrician first and follow his suggestions. However, there are several good choices to consider, including rice cereal (which is easy to digest), very ripe, finely mashed banana or pear, and applesauce. Some doctors recommend introducing cooked, puréed strained vegetables before fruits, as they are blander. If you decide to do this, start with the "yellow" vegetables like carrots, potatoes, squash, and sweet potatoes. (In the next couple of months you may add beets, peas, spinach, green beans, asparagus, cauliflower, and avocados.)

Should your baby refuse to take a food you are giving him for the first time, don't agonize over it or insist. Try something else. Once he is more used to coping with solids, he will probably be much more amenable toward previously rejected foods.

If you started with rice cereal, for instance, and your child has tolerated it well for several days, introduce him to oatmeal. Don't use the adult variety but one prepared especially for infants. If he tolerates oatmeal well, follow it with barley cereal.

When introducing any new food, give your child the same food for at least four days. Once you see that he is tolerating it well, and he has no allergic reaction to it, you may introduce something else. In the event of intolerance or allergy to a specific food, you may find one or more of the following symptoms: change in amount and smell of food baby spits up, frequent and runny stools, rashes, fever, or vomiting. Call your doctor immediately should any of these symptoms occur and work out a special diet with him.

Feed solids only once a day initially; in the morning is best. After a week of cereal for breakfast, add an evening feeding, too. Cereal should now be fed to your little one daily until he is at least eighteen months old. Remember, though, nursing or the bottle is still going to be his main source of food, and it will be at least another month before he is eating a complete meal.

About four weeks after introducing cereals, fruit, and vegetables, meat may be added to the diet. As your baby drinks less milk, meat will provide most of his protein, iron, and the B-complex vitamins. All meats should be finely ground or strained so they can be easily swallowed. Use chicken, veal, turkey, lamb, beef, and liver. Pork, although very high in protein, is also very high in fat and should not be given too often. When it is served, it must be very well cooked.

Here are some other guidelines to keep in mind while weaning your baby:

- Don't feed excessive amounts of juice. This may decrease your baby's intake of milk or formula, which is still his most important nutrient.
- Since an insufficiency of iron in your baby's body is one reason to start him on solids at six months, give him egg yolk, one of nature's best sources of iron for an infant to start with. Hard-boil an egg, remove the yolk, and mix it with some cereal, a banana, or a little milk. The reason for not giving your child egg white at this age is the risk of an allergic reaction.
- Don't add sugar or honey to any cereal. If your baby doesn't get used to sweet tastes, he won't miss them.

· When you decide to introduce fruits or vegetables into the diet, use the same procedure as for cereal, only one fruit or vegetable at a time. Bananas must be very ripe—the skin should be speckled brown—as unripe bananas are difficult to digest. Other fruits you may give your baby at this time are cooked apples, pears, prunes, peaches, and apricots.

· Most fruits, and especially prunes, have a mild laxative effect, so keep this in mind if your baby is constipated. You can increase or decrease the amount of fruit you give, depending on the frequency and consistency of your baby's bowel movements. Of course, there will be a change in baby's bowel movements once you start feeding him solids. This is normal. A breast-fed baby will probably have more frequent movements once he is started on solids, although this is not necessarily true of a bottle-fed baby.

· Don't put your child to bed with a bottle of juice or milk once his teeth start coming through. This may quite possibly promote cavities. If he needs the comfort of sucking occasionally after you have put him to bed, give him a bottle of plain boiled water.

SUMMARY: WHEN TO INTRODUCE SOLIDS

Six Months

Juices: Apple, apricot nectar, carrot (in moderation), pear, and prune
Fruits: Cooked apples, apricots, nectarines, peaches, pears, plums, and prunes; raw, very ripe bananas, nectarines, and peaches
Vegetables: Carrots, green beans, peas, wax beans, and winter squash (all cooked)
Miscellaneous: Cereals, except wheat; egg yolk

Seven Months

Juices: Cherry
Fruits: Cooked pitted cherries; raw, very ripe pears
Vegetables: Artichoke hearts, asparagus tips, broccoli, celery,
                 corn, potatoes, summer squash, tomatoes, and yams
                 (all cooked)
Miscellaneous: Cheese; meats

Eight Months

Fruits: Ripe apricots, plums, and prunes (all raw)
Vegetables: Beets, greens, legumes (beans, peas, lentils), lima
                 beans, okra, parsnips, peppers, rutabaga, spinach,
                 and turnips (all cooked)

Nine Months

Juices: Cranberry, grape, grapefruit, guava nectar, lemon,
                 mango nectar, orange, papaya nectar, pineapple, and
                 tomato

Although citrus fruits (oranges, grapefruit, lemons, limes) can be
allergenic, they are an excellent source of vitamin C. Therefore,
citrus juices may be introduced at this time. Dilute them with an
equal amount of water until you are satisfied that your baby shows
no sign of allergic reaction.

Fruits: Avocado, cantaloupe, pitted cherries, guava, kiwi
                 fruit, mangoes, persimmons, and pineapple (all raw)
Vegetables: Brussels sprouts, cabbage, cauliflower, eggplant,
                 kohlrabi, mushrooms, and onions (all cooked); raw
                 tomatoes
Miscellaneous: Wheat products

Twelve Months

Fruits: Berries, figs, grapes, grapefruit, and oranges (all
                     raw)
Vegetables: Cucumber (peeled)
Miscellaneous: Egg white; fish
Notes: (1) Never boil juices. Heat destroys vitamin C.
                     (2) Except where specified raw, all vegetables should
                          be cooked during the first year.

HOMEMADE BABY FOODS

Why make your own baby foods when they can be purchased
from the market? There are many advantages, some of which are:

· They are freshly made and more nutritious.
· They cost less than commercial baby foods.
· They can be made to different consistencies, to suit your baby's
  needs. Many commercial baby foods are too thin for older infants.
· They can be familiar foods, prepared without excess water or
  salt, sugar, starches, or tapioca (which are often added to store-
  bought baby foods).
· Baby is introduced to foods that taste more like the table foods
  he will soon be eating.
· Homemade baby food may take only a little longer to prepare
  than heating a jar of the commercial kind. Many baby foods can
  be prepared in a few minutes.

Here are some points to remember when preparing baby foods at
home:

· Clean hands, utensils, and work surfaces are essential. Wash all
  equipment thoroughly in hot soapy water and rinse well before
  using. Take apart food grinders, blenders, and processors after

each use and wash them thoroughly. Dry each part before putting appliance together again.

· Use fresh, good-quality food that has been stored in clean containers at correct refrigerator temperatures (no higher than 40°F [4°C]). Vegetables (especially spinach) should be fresh and used within two days of purchase.

· Wash all fruits, vegetables, fish, meats (except for red or ground meats), and poultry before preparing.

· Do not overcook vegetables or fruits. Either cook them in a small amount of water in a covered pan or, whenever possible, steam them, saving the liquid for thinning the food. Cook just until tender.

· Put leftovers in clean covered containers and refrigerate immediately. Use within one or two days.

· To freeze baby food, pour portions into individual plastic ice cube trays. When frozen, pop food cubes out of containers into a plastic bag, seal, and store in freezer. To serve, remove a cube and melt over low heat in a small saucepan. Freezer temperature should be 0°F (−18°C) or lower. Use frozen baby foods within two months.

· Heat only the quantity of food you need for each feeding whenever possible. Leftovers from the feeding dish should be discarded.

· When preparing family recipes for baby, remove his portion before adding salt, sugar, or spicy seasonings.

EQUIPMENT (SEE ALSO BASIC EQUIPMENT LIST WHICH FOLLOWS):
Infant foods can be prepared with many kinds of equipment, from a simple fork or a sieve or strainer, to an expensive food processor. Food mills, baby-food grinders, and blenders may also be used, and they work well. If using a wire strainer, be sure it is in very good condition so that there is no danger of small pieces of mesh getting into the food.

PREPARING CEREALS:
Most infants start out with precooked baby cereals, fortified with iron. Those are simply prepared by stirring dry cereal into the appropriate quantity of warmed liquid.

Health-food stores now carry a wide variety of unrefined, quick-cooking cereals such as oat, cream of rye, cream of soya, cream of wheat, cream of rice, and corn grits, none of which take more than a few minutes to cook. Also available are whole-grain cereals, which usually require approximately thirty minutes to cook (and may need to be puréed before being served to infants). These cereals include rolled oats, millet, barley flakes, rice, and cracked wheat. Cooking directions can be found on the packages. But remember that these cereals contain much less iron than commercial infant cereals, and that breast milk and cow's milk contain very little iron. From the age of six months, an infant may require additional iron in his diet, and this should be checked with a pediatrician.

PREPARING VEGETABLES:
Wash and peel vegetables, cut into small even-sized pieces, and steam or boil in a small amount of water until soft. (Carrots should be scrubbed, not peeled, to retain nutrients.)

Most vegetables cook in a few minutes and then can be pressed through a fine strainer, mashed with a fork, or puréed. Remove any coarse pieces or skin. If using a blender or food processor, mix ½ cup of cooked, diced vegetables with ¼ cup of liquid (milk, vegetable or meat broth formula, or juice). Blend until smooth.

PREPARING FRUITS:
Prepare and cook fresh fruits as for vegetables, preferably peeling fruits *after* cooking. Bananas should be ripe, never cooked, and need only be mashed with a fork to serve. Stew dried fruits in a little water until soft, then purée in the cooking liquid for infants, or mash for older children. Pitted dried fruits can be offered as a finger food at twelve months without being soaked or cooked.

PREPARING MEATS AND FISH:
Cut lean raw beef, lamb, liver, veal, chicken, turkey, or fish into small pieces, then steam, bake, broil, stew, or sauté; then purée or grind meat in a food mill or grinder, blender, or processor. After meat or fish is cooked, liquid may be used for thinning.

Once an infant has several teeth, the consistency of foods should be coarser but still tender. Mash fruits and vegetables, finely chop meats, progressing to finely diced meats.

SAVING TIME:

Preparing baby foods may seem too time-consuming for working parents. But keeping in mind the child's well-being, compromises can be worked out to make it possible to prepare nutritious home-made baby foods quickly and easily for later use. Home-cooked vegetables, fruits, and eggs can be made very quickly and served with commercial baby meat dishes that would take a little longer to prepare yourself.

To take on outings or for baby-sitters, small lunch-box thermos bottles are ideal for storing soft steamed vegetables and fruits. The food can either be mashed prior to being put in the thermos or just before serving.

Several kinds of vegetables can be steamed together, some to serve now, some for later. When an infant can cope with more textured foods, use several small thermos "pots" for pasta, rice, beans, cottage cheese, yogurt, fruit, meats, or vegetables. In this way, it is possible for your baby to be given the nutritious foods you have prepared even if you cannot be there to feed him yourself.

BASIC EQUIPMENT LIST (ONE OR MORE OF THE FOLLOWING):

Small sieve or strainer
Food mill or grinder
Food processor or blender
Potato masher
Steamer basket or saucepan with steamer
Lidded saucepan
Egg poacher (for reheating leftovers)
Small covered containers for leftovers
Individual ice cube trays for freezing food (optional)
Storage bags for freezing (optional)
Measuring spoons, 1 teaspoon and 1 tablespoon sizes
Paring knife
Vegetable brush

Babies' and Toddlers' Balanced Menus

BREAKFASTS

In the first year of your baby's life, breakfasts are rather simple, with the emphasis on cereals. The most suitable cereals are rice, oat, barley, rye, and millet. The specially prepared infant cereals available in supermarkets are best initially, as they are fortified with iron and do not contain sugar or salt. Breast milk, formula, or cow's milk can be used to mix the cereals.

In addition to cereals, serve mashed banana, applesauce, or puréed, cooked fresh pears, peaches, or apricots. These fruits can be mixed with cereal or offered separately. If you don't give your baby fruit, give him instead a cup of apple, pear, apricot, or cherry juice. One egg *yolk*, hard-boiled or scrambled with a tablespoon of milk, will make this a nutritionally complete breakfast.

After twelve months, breakfasts become more diversified. The menus that follow will give you some ideas to supplement with your own.

When I started my daughter on wheat cereals, I found two varieties at the health-food store that were instant favorites. The first was a Swiss cereal containing rye, oat, and millet flakes, whole wheat, dried shredded dates, apples, bananas, ground almonds, and wheat germ. I served it cold with milk. The second was a sprouted-wheat cereal with bananas which also contained oats and barley. Later I switched to regular oatmeal, and I tried other cereals such

as grits, Roman Meal, and Malt-O-Meal, which my little one enjoyed. Your baby will choose his own favorites. Introduce him to
many kinds but always read the labels first to ensure the cereals do
not contain sugar or salt. Stay away from ready-to-eat commercial
cereals, as most of them contain enormous amounts of sugar (some
over 50 percent) and large quantities of salt (up to 375 milligrams
per ounce). Many of these cereals also contain BHA and BHT,
antioxidants that help preserve freshness.

Your baby should have cooked cereal at least once a day until
he is eighteen months old. For a special treat you can occasionally
replace cereal with pancakes (I found a soy-wheat pancake mix that
is naturally sweet, as it contains dried apples and pear juice), or
whole wheat toast spread with mashed banana or cheese.

After twelve months is also the time to introduce brewer's yeast
into your infant's juice at breakfast. It is a superior source of the
natural B-complex vitamins. Start with ⅛ teaspoon and slowly increase the quantity to 1 teaspoon.

A few final facts on cereals that are important to keep in mind:
All cereals contain some protein, approximately 2 to 6 grams per
ounce, but are low in lysine, an essential amino acid. However, the
addition of milk, which is rich in lysine, will make the cereal protein complete. Governmental dietary guidelines recommend that
Americans reduce their intake of fats and consume more complex
carbohydrates such as corn, wheat, rice, oats, and barley, the main
ingredients of cereals. According to these guidelines, a bowl of *unsweetened* cereal is healthier than fried eggs and bacon.

12 Months Onward

See Index for recipes.

Soft-boiled egg	Sprouted cereal with milk
Oatmeal with Applesauce* and milk	Poached egg
½ cup orange juice with 1 tsp. brewer's yeast	Orange slices

Millet Cereal* with Applesauce*
Scrambled egg
½ cup orange juice with 1 tsp.
brewer's yeast

———

Roman Meal cereal with milk
½ fresh peach, sliced

———

Scrambled egg
½ slice whole wheat bread and
butter with banana slices
1 cup milk

———

Cornmeal Mush* with milk
½ banana
1 cup warm milk with carob

———

Hominy grits with milk
Poached egg
Small piece of melon

———

Swiss cereal with milk
Soft-boiled egg
¼ cored, peeled apple

———

Small soy-wheat pancake with
butter and Applesauce*
Apricot Breakfast Shake*

Scrambled egg
Barley Cereal with milk
½ cup orange juice with 1 tsp.
brewer's yeast

———

Malt-O-Meal with milk
Poached egg
¼ pear, peeled and cored

———

Scrambled egg
Small soy-wheat pancake with
butter
Orange Milk Whip*

———

Oatmeal with fresh strawberries
and milk
Soft-boiled egg

———

Swiss cereal with milk
Poached egg
½ cup fresh carrot juice

———

Bread Pudding* with raisins
½ cup orange juice with 1 tsp.
brewer's yeast

———

Swedish Potato Pancake* with
Applesauce*
1 cup milk

Rice cereal with milk
Soft-boiled egg
½ apple or pear, peeled and
cored

———

Hominy grits with butter and
milk
½ banana
Poached egg
½ cup apple juice with 1 tsp.
brewer's yeast

Rye cereal with milk
Scrambled egg
Orange Milk Whip*

———

Cornmeal Mush* with milk
Orange slices
Apricot Shake*

———

Scrambled egg
½ slice wheat toast with nut
butter
½ cup orange juice with 1 tsp.
brewer's yeast

LUNCH AND DINNER MENUS

The menus that follow are samples that provide nutritious and balanced meals. Lunches and dinners are interchangeable and may be served either at midday or in the evening. Give your baby ½ tablespoonful of food from each food group at six months of age and progress to 1 tablespoonful at around a year. If your baby's appetite is larger, increase the amounts equally from the four food groups to satisfy it.

All the menus for the first twelve months you can continue to use later. Only the quantity and consistency of the food change, depending on baby's age and the number of teeth he has.

I usually served my child only one meat dish a day, and many days I served no meat at all, making up the protein requirement with egg yolk, cheese, yogurt, milk, and rice and beans. Egg was part of her daily diet, but if I planned on giving her one for lunch or dinner, she didn't have one for breakfast. By her first birthday she had shown no signs of allergies, so I fed her the food I prepared for the rest of my family. There was some increase in her salt intake, but it was very moderate. For our welfare as well as my daughter's, I have cut down drastically on salt in our diets.

Many of the meals listed here can be prepared very quickly. Others, such as those comprising soups, casseroles, beans, and roasts, I made on my days off and used the leftovers on working days. And of course as time went on, Mirabai had her small share of what I cooked for the rest of the family.

Vegetables are always more nutritious and attractive if freshly steamed as needed. Steaming takes only a few minutes. (Peas, potatoes, beets, and other root vegetables, however, may be cooked in boiling water.)

Menu dishes requiring a special recipe are marked with an asterisk (*). See the Index for page numbers. As noted in the menus, all meals should be accompanied by nursing, formula, or milk.

A steamer and a blender or food processor are fine investments if you don't already have them. I strongly recommend using the steamer for your own as well as your baby's foods. An egg poacher is also useful for reheating small portions of up to three or four different foods quickly and easily.

When cooking fruit, I prepared and puréed enough for three or four days, then refrigerated it in sterilized baby jars. Bottles can be sterilized in a dishwasher, or by boiling them in a saucepan of water for five minutes.

I did not freeze my baby foods because it usually took as long to heat them as it did to prepare them from scratch. I also felt that some of the flavor was lost by freezing. This, however, is an individual preference and freezing should not be discounted if you find it useful.

Seven Months

*Note: Each meal should be accompanied
by nursing, formula, or milk.*

Creamed summer squash
Cottage cheese
Mashed pear

———

Vegetable Custard*
Rice and Prune Pudding*

———

Puréed beef
Creamed string beans
Sweet Potato and Apple
Purée*

———

Ricotta cheese
Creamed carrots
Mashed banana

———

Puréed veal
Mashed potato
Mashed peas
Applesauce*

———

Creamed asparagus
Cottage cheese
Mashed peeled nectarine

Puréed chicken
Mashed sweet potato
Fruit Compote*

———

Mashed sautéed tofu
Mashed asparagus with
Parmesan cheese
Fruit Custard*

———

Baked Acorn or Summer
Squash*
Cottage cheese with puréed
cherries

———

Puréed carrots
Rice
Plain yogurt with mashed
peach

———

Mashed carrots and peas
Pastina
Fruit Custard*

———

Puréed turkey
Puréed corn
Mashed pitted plum and
banana

Mashed carrots and peas
Cooked Barley,* mashed
Plain yogurt with mashed
cherries

————

Puréed lamb
Puréed wax beans
Puréed prune

————

Rice and scrambled egg yolk
Mashed broccoli
Plain yogurt with mashed plum

————

Puréed turkey
Mashed potato
Stewed tomato
Cooked puréed apricot

————

Mashed tofu
Mashed carrots and green
beans
Plain yogurt with mashed pear

Puréed lamb
Mashed potatoes and peas
Rice and Apricot Pudding*

————

Puréed chicken
Creamed carrots
Boiled potato, mashed with
butter

————

Cottage Cheese with Scrambled
Egg* (egg yolk only)
Cooked skinned tomato
Mashed banana

————

Puréed beef
Creamed broccoli
Carrot Apple Purée*

————

Puréed veal
Baked Acorn Squash*
Plum Yum*

Eight Months

*Note: Each meal should be accompanied
by nursing, formula, or milk.*

Sautéed Calf's Liver*
Creamed spinach
Mashed yam
ABC Dessert*

Lentil Roast*
Rice Pudding*

Leftover Turkey Soup* with
vegetables
Peachy Pudding*

————

Small White Beans* (with
tomato and parsley)
Cottage Cheese Pudding*

————

Pastinas with Peas*
Ricotta cheese with mashed
peach

————

Vegetables Tofu*
Mashed Peas
Plain yogurt with mashed pear

————

Yam Soup*
Mashed pinto beans
Rice and Prune Pudding*

————

Puréed beef
Steamed yellow squash,
mashed
Creamed string beans
Applesauce*

————

Lentil and Banana Mash*
Rice Royal*
Plain yogurt

Puréed chicken
Mashed Rutabaga and Carrots*
Mashed banana

————

Stelline with Cottage Cheese*
Cream of Tomato Soup*
Fruit Compote*

————

Vegetable Custard*
Mashed apricots and tofu

————

Beans and Broccoli with Stars*
Carrots and Beets with Apple*

————

Tofu-Rice Casserole*
Baked Acorn Squash*
Grape Divine*

————

Macaroni Marinara*
Tofu with Egg*
Carrot Apple Purée*

————

Puréed turkey
Baked sweet potato, mashed
Mashed pear

————

Lentil and Potato Stew*
Broiled Tomato*
Rice Pudding*

Mashed broccoli and carrots
Rice
Ricotta cheese with mashed
peach

———

Sautéed Calf's Liver*
Sweet Potato and Apple
Purée*

———

Puréed Kidney with Carrots*
Frijoles II*
Apple Mist*

———

Mashed Cuban Black Beans*
(and rice)
Carrot Apple Purée*
Plain yogurt

Shepherd's Pie*
Mashed peas
Mashed banana

———

Puréed split peas
Heavenly Potato*
Mashed Rutabaga and Carrots*
Plum Yum*

———

Peruvian Bean Purée*
Cottage Cheese Pudding*
Banana Raita*

———

Stuffed Zucchini with Apricot*
Baked potato
Stewed Plums* (with yogurt)

Nine Months

*Note: Each meal should be accompanied
by nursing, formula, or milk.*

Zucchini Mushroom Pie*
Sautéed ground beef
Papaya slices

———

Spinach Yogurt Bake*
Baked potato
Peeled pear slices

Homemade Chicken Soup*
(with pastina and carrots)
Bread Pudding*

———

Beef, Bean, and Macaroni
Casserole*
Brussels Sprouts and Carrots in
Lemon Butter*
Mango slices

Cheesy Baked Squash *
Mashed potato
Peeled pitted peach slices

————

Finely shredded turkey
Rice
Green Peas with Pineapple *

————

Peruvian Potatoes *
Carrots and Beets with Apple *
Plain yogurt

————

Stelline with Marinara Sauce *
Ricotta cheese with apricot

————

Chicken Fricassee *
Cauliflower and carrots,
chopped
Boiled potato
Pineapple pieces

————

Stuffed Tomato Treat *
Rice
Tropical Treat *

————

Cooked Barley * (with ground
beef)
Chopped carrots with parsley
Melon slices

Shredded chicken
Yam and Carrot Balls with
Raisins *

————

Cheese and Lentil Loaf *
Avocado and Papaya Salad *

————

Bean and Cheese Melt *
Steamed chopped spinach
Yogurt Ambrosia *

————

Broiled ground lamb
Mashed yam
Heart of artichoke
Orange Cloud *

————

Broiled Liver Patties *
Mashed potato
Creamy Turnip *
Mango slices

————

Stuffed Bell Peppers *
Peruvian Bean Purée *
Bread Pudding *

————

Tofu and Cauliflower *
Avocado and tomato slices
Banana Coconut Pudding *

Broiled ground beef
Baked sweet potato
Steamed broccoli
Peeled pitted nectarine slices

———

Finely chopped turkey
Steamed chopped carrots
Rice and Pineapple Pudding*

———

Norwegian Lamb and
Cabbage*
Boiled potato
Cantaloupe slices

———

Tofu-Rice Casserole*
Tomato Eggplant Cups*
Banana Raita*

Puréed Kidneys with Carrots*
Sweet Potato and Apple
Purée*

———

Zucchini Beef Skillet*
Carrots and Beets with Apple*

———

Eggplant Parmesan*
Rice
Plain yogurt with papaya slices

———

Frijoles I* (refried beans)
Yam and Carrot Balls with
Raisins*
Rice Royal*
Plain yogurt with peach slices

———

Peruvian Potatoes*
Baked Acorn Squash*
Rice Pudding*

Ten Months

*Note: Each meal should be accompanied
by nursing, formula, or milk.*

Mushroom Tofu Stroganoff*
Rice Royal*
ABC Dessert*

Karin's Health Soup*
Slice whole wheat toast
Yogurt Ambrosia*

Baked Mostaccioli*
Avocado and Papaya Salad*

————

Split Pea Soup*
Slice whole wheat bread
Rice Pudding*

————

Roast Lamb and Potatoes*
Green Peas with Pineapple*

————

Soy Potato Burgers*
Creamy Turnip*
Kiwi fruit slices

————

Leftover Lamb with Beans*
Mashed Rutabaga and Carrots*
Sliced fresh pear

————

Cream of Broccoli Soup*
Slice whole wheat bread
Cottage Cheese Pudding*

————

Scalloped Potatoes with Ham*
Asparagus with Parmesan
Cheese*
Apple Gel*

————

Vegetables Tofu*
Bean and Cheese Melt*
Broiled Banana*

Chicken Soup with Speck*
Slice whole wheat bread
Tropical Treat*

————

Meat Cakes*
Sweet Potato Scramble*
Mashed avocado and banana

————

Tofu-Cheese Soufflé*
Cooked beets and green beans
Sliced apple

————

Liver Loaf*
Yam and Carrot Balls with
Raisins*
Cantaloupe slices

————

Syrian Lentil Soup*
Slice whole wheat bread
Stewed Plums* (with plain
yogurt)

————

Ground Veal Patties*
Cooked beets and Brussels
sprouts
Rice and Apricot Pudding*

————

Cream of Tomato Soup*
Sweet and Savory Eggplant*
Rice
Peach slices

Meatballs *
Heavenly Potato *
Green Peas with Pineapple *

———

Stelline with Cottage Cheese *
Steamed broccoli
Avocado and tomato slices
Baked Apple *

———

Finely diced chicken
Mashed potato
Chopped spinach
Banana Coconut Pudding *

Yam Soup *
Corn Bread *
Avocado and Papaya Salad *
Banana Raita *

———

Puréed Kidneys with Carrot *
Small White Beans *
Grape Divine *

———

Tomato Eggplant Cups *
Peruvian Potatoes *
Cottage cheese with mango
slices

———

Cold Cream of Avocado Soup *
Vegetable Rice Casserole *
Poached Apple *

Eleven Months

*Note: Each meal should be accompanied
by nursing, formula, or milk.*

Tofu and Cauliflower *
Green Peas with Pineapple *
Apple Gel *

———

Meatballs *
Mashed potato
Chopped carrots and green
beans
Pear Surprise *

Lima Beans *
Rice
Sweet Potato Scramble *
Persimmon slices

———

Sautéed Calf's Liver *
Baked potato
Chopped steamed broccoli
Apple slices

Yellow Pea Soup with
Vegetables and Sausage*
Banana

———

Stelline with Cottage Cheese*
Steamed carrots and peas
Yogurt Ambrosia*

———

Baked Chicken with Tarragon*
Creamed corn
Rice
Watermelon

———

Chicken Soup with Speck*
Avocado and tomato slices
Orange Soufflé*

———

Millet Soufflé*
Stuffed Tomato Treat*
Cold Apricot Soup*

———

Veal sausage, chopped
Swedish Potato Pancakes* with
Applesauce*
Mashed Rutabaga and Carrots*

———

Cheese and Lentil Loaf*
Squash with Green Beans*
Cottage cheese with peach
slices

Baked Liver with Cider*
Baked sweet potato
Creamed spinach
Nectarine slices

———

Vegetables Tofu*
Rice
Brussels Sprouts and Carrots in
Lemon Butter*
Kiwi Kwiki*

———

Groundnut Chicken Stew*
Rice
Broiled Banana*

———

Sweet Potato Scramble*
Rice and Apricot Pudding*

———

Tofu-Rice Casserole*
Stuffed Mushrooms*
Broiled Tomato*
Apple Mist*

———

Broiled Liver Patties*
Pasta e Fagioli* (macaroni and
beans)
Steamed spinach
Cantaloupe slices

Bean, Rice, and Vegetable
Soup*
Peachy Pudding*

———

Lentil Soup*
Rice Royal*
Summer Delight*

———

Piselli con Uova* (peas with
egg)
Rice
Slice whole wheat bread
Banana Raita*

Asparagus Omelet*
Steamed zucchini and carrots
Sautéed potato
Cold Melon Soup*

———

Rice with Cheese*
Carrots and Beets with Apple*
ABC Dessert*

———

Cottage Cheese and Noodle
Casserole*
Avocado and tomato slices
Slice whole wheat bread
Applesauce* (with plain
yogurt)

Twelve Months

Note: Each meal should be accompanied by milk.

Small sticks of cold ham
Garbanzo Bean Purée*
Pita Bread*
Cold, cooked carrot sticks
Figs in Yogurt*

———

Cabbage Rolls*
Green Beans with Walnuts*
Apricot Soup*

———

Oven-Baked Fish*
Baked potato
Mashed steamed carrots
Fresh pear slices

Spanakopita*
Carrot Raita*
Fresh pineapple pieces

———

Fried Tofu with Mushrooms*
Heavenly Potato*
Fresh peach slices

———

Cholent* (meat, bean, and
vegetable soup)
Challah* (bread)
Sliced seeded orange

Broiled Sturgeon *
Boiled potato
Steamed, chopped spinach
Strawberries

———

Meat Cakes *
Bulgur Pilaff *
Cauliflower with Avocado-
Tahini Dressing *
Tangerine segments

———

Steamed Salmon Loaf *
Mashed potato
Steamed chopped broccoli
Fresh raspberries

———

Pineapple Chicken Supreme *
Rice
Plain yogurt

———

Fiske Kaker * (Norwegian
fishcakes)
Boiled potato
Cooked beets
Pear Delight *

———

Semolina Primavera *
Ricotta cheese with
strawberries

Oven-Baked Fish *
Baked sweet potato
Peas
Fruit Compote *

———

Chicken and Papaya Soup *
Slice whole wheat bread
Kiwi fruit slices

———

Fish with Fresh Tomato *
Mashed potato
Avocado slices
Strawberry Banana Mold *

———

Macaroni Marinara *
Steamed broccoli and carrots
Rice Pudding *

———

Stuffed Bell Peppers *
Avocado and Papaya Salad *
Cottage Cheese Pudding *

———

Sole Meunière *
Baked potato
Creamy Turnip *
Watermelon pieces

———

Arabian Stew *
Pita Bread *
Persian melon slices

Spinach and Potato Casserole *
Slice whole wheat bread
Yogurt Delight *

———

Simple Fish and Vegetables *
Rice
Cantaloupe slices

———

Ham Omelet *
Asparagus with Parmesan
Cheese *
Tropical Treat *

Lentil Roast *
Stuffed Tomato Treat *
Cranberry Cubes *

———

Poached Fish with Yogurt
Sauce *
Mashed potato
Green beans
Fresh Fruit Salad *

———

Celery Soup *
Slice whole wheat bread
Peruvian Potatoes *
Orange segments

Thirteen to Seventeen Months

Note: Each meal should be accompanied by milk.

Beef, Bean, and Macaroni
Casserole *
Okra
Persimmon with Grapes *

———

Egg Nest *
Slice whole wheat bread
Strawberry Fruit Soup *

———

Baked Haddock and Potatoes *
Steamed broccoli
Tomato and cucumber salad
Homemade Apple Pie *

Poached Egg with Spinach *
Rice Royal *
Apple Strawberry Parfait *

———

Fish and Rice Casserole *
Bread Pudding *

———

Black-eyed Peas and Rice *
Yam and Carrot Balls with
Raisins *
Fresh Fruit Salad *

Shrimp and Okra Stew*
Rice
Raspberry Tarte*

———

Ricotta Cheese Pancakes*
Pineapple Coleslaw*
Plain yogurt

———

Tuna Fish Casserole*
Steamed green beans
Fruit Compote*

———

Greek Lamb Stew*
Cucumber Salad*
Orange segments

———

Haddock with Egg Butter*
Boiled potato
Steamed carrots
Peach slices

———

Summer Salad*
Pita Bread* (with melted
cheese)

———

Fettucine*
Avocado and Papaya Salad*
Cottage cheese with
strawberries

Chicken Breasts with Lime
Butter*
Asparagus with Parmesan
Cheese*
Plain yogurt with papaya slices

———

Veal Scaloppine*
Carrot Raita*
Poached Apple*

———

Seafood Salad*
Melon Berry Melba*

———

Lentils Indian Style*
Chapatis*
Indian Vegetables with Rice*
Banana Raita*

———

Baked Potatoes with Salmon
Sauce*
Carrot Raita*
Cranberry Cubes*

———

Zucchini Beef Skillet*
Macaroni Marinara*
Pear Surprise*

———

White Bean and Cabbage
Soup*
Slice whole wheat bread
Rice Pudding*

Scalloped Potatoes with Ham*
Baked Acorn Squash*
Nectarine slices

Calamari*
Rice
Tangerine segments

———

Vegetable Barley Soup*
Slice whole wheat bread
Ricotta cheese and fresh or
canned pineapple pieces

Eighteen Months to Two Years

Note: Each meal should be accompanied by milk.

Black Bean Soup*
Tabbouleh Salad*
Avocado and Papaya Salad*
Plain yogurt

Creamy Halibut Bake*
Baked potato
Fresh steamed asparagus tips
Fresh strawberries

———

Stir-fried Squid with Pea
Pods*
Rice
Persimmon

Cornish Game Hens with
Grapes and Orange Butter*
Rice
Steamed broccoli
Pear slices

———

Baked Ham in Vegetable
Juice*
Baked yam
Green Beans with Walnuts*
Fresh pineapple pieces

Italian Rice and Avocado
Salad*
Summer Delight*

———

Macaroni Salad*
Slice whole wheat bread
Baked Apple*

Fiskepudding* (Norwegian fish
pudding)
Boiled potato
Steamed asparagus tips and
carrots
Apple slices

Quesadilla* (tortilla with
cheese)
Cold Cream of Avocado Soup*
Rice and Apricot Pudding*

———

Baked Sea Bass Oriental*
Rice
Stir-fried Chinese pea pods and
mushrooms
Orange segments

———

Roast Chicken in Tomato
Sauce*
Mashed potato
Peas
Nectarine slices

———

Cheese Enchiladas*
Frijoles I* (refried beans)
Rice
Kiwi fruit slices

———

Shrimp with Almond Yogurt
Sauce*
Steamed spinach
Rice
Fresh fig

Veal Scaloppine*
Sautéed potato
Cantaloupe slices

———

Halloween Stew*
Persimmon and Black Grapes*

———

Avocado with cooked shrimp
Half hard-boiled egg and tomato slices
on lettuce leaf
Slice whole wheat bread
Apricot Soup*

———

Cuban Chicken* (with carrots
and potatoes)
Fresh Fruit Salad*

———

Sautéed Calf's Liver*
Mashed Rutabaga and Carrots*
Baked potato
ABC Dessert*

———

Asparagus Omelet*
Lentil Soup*
Fresh pitted plum

———

Salmon Soufflé*
Cauliflower with Avocado-
Tahini Dressing*
Fresh pitted cherries

Boned Chicken Chinese Style*   Cream of Tomato Soup* (with
    (with bean sprouts,   macaroni)
mushrooms, and snow peas)   Slice whole wheat bread
            Rice   Lentil and Banana Mash*
Banana Coconut Pudding*   Figs in Yogurt*

———

Pot-au-Feu*
Norwegian Birthday Cake*

SNACKS AND FINGER FOODS

From about eight months of age, your baby will probably be able
to use his thumb and fingers to pick up pieces of food. Although he
may have only a couple of teeth, this is a good time to introduce
finger foods. These will be "gummed," a little will end up in the
tummy, and the remainder will be spat out. Chewing is the first
step in your baby's development toward independent feeding.

Start him off with a piece of banana, a rice or rye cracker, thin
strips of cheese or avocado, or well-cooked pieces of carrot, potato,
apple, or asparagus tips. As your little one acquires more teeth, the
list of foods will get longer. After nine months, add wheat bread,
wheat crackers, melon, soft raw pitted apricots and prunes. When
baby is one year, the fruits you have been cooking, such as apples,
pears, and peaches, can be given to him fresh. They must be peeled,
cored, and stoned where necessary, and cut into several pieces.
Fingers of bread can be covered with liver pâté, cream cheese,
apple or banana, thinly sliced cheese, nut butters, mashed carrots,
or applesauce.

Make your child's snacks healthy, with food values similar to
those of a regular meal. As my daughter ate well at each meal, I
usually didn't offer her snacks, although I would give her a cup of
milk or juice between meals. If I didn't have time to prepare a hot

meal, or she indicated that she was hungry between meals, I made a snack which combined the necessary protein, fats, carbohydrates, vitamins, and minerals. This meant including something from each one of the four food groups listed below:

· *Meat Group:* fish, poultry, eggs, legumes (dried beans, peas, and lentils), nut butters, and tofu
· *Milk Group:* milk, yogurt, and cheeses
· *Fruits and Vegetables Group:* citrus fruits, fleshy fruits, leafy vegetables, green and yellow vegetables, and tubers (potatoes, yams, and other root vegetables)
· *Bread and Cereals Group:* pasta, rice, cereals, cornmeal, oats, grits, and baked goods

Following is a list of snacks which can be easily and quickly prepared from foods that are probably in your refrigerator. I have separated them into three age groups for easy reference.

8 to 12 Months of Age

Hard-boiled egg yolk, ground beef, chicken, turkey, or lamb made into little meat cakes (see page 217)

Mozzarella, jack, cheddar, Swiss, or string cheese cut into 1 × 3 strips; cream cheese on a cracker; yogurt; cottage cheese

Apple, pear, or peach slices, all peeled, cored, and steamed until soft; prunes and dried apricots, soaked until soft; ripe bananas

Broccoli, asparagus tips, beets, carrots, cauliflower, peas, string beans, potatoes, turnips, sweet potatoes, cut into 1 × 3 pieces (except peas, of course!) and steamed; ripe avocado slices

Rye, oat, and rice cereals; toast or crackers. Bread can be hardened for teething by cutting into finger-size pieces and baking in preheated 150° to 200° oven for 15 to 20 minutes.

12 Months to 18 Months

Add to the above:

Whole egg; nut butters; fish sticks; diced or sliced poultry

Fresh fruits, including melon, oranges, figs, mangoes, papaya, kiwi fruit, strawberries; all other fruits previously cooked

Fresh vegetables, including lettuce, mushroom slices, and cut-up tomatoes; raw broccoli and cauliflower pieces, shredded carrots, and raw string beans

Wheat toast, bread, crackers, and breadsticks. (Make open-face sandwiches with applesauce, mashed fruits, melted cheese, or cream cheese.)

18 Months Onward

Milk and fruit shakes, fruit popsicles, kefir. *Sample menus:*

Apple wedges with peanut butter. Kefir.

Slice of wheat bread with cheese. Shredded carrot. Juice.

Cooked egg with slice of wheat bread and butter. Juice.

Wheat crackers. Kefir with grated apple.

Open-face banana sandwich on whole wheat bread. Milk.

Mirabai's Diary from Six Months to Her Second Birthday

Mid-September (6 Months)

Mirabai is six months old today and we are going to celebrate by starting her on solids. I purchased some precooked infant rice cereal, a little of which I mixed with warm milk until it became a semiliquid. I tested the cereal carefully with my lips to make sure it was not too hot. Mirabai was enveloped in a bib stating that "I Love Daddy" and adorned with hearts, pandas, and bluebirds. To complete our exciting initiation into solids, I used a little silver dish that came from Norway a long time ago. However, I bought a modern baby spoon with a white plastic coating over the bowl part.

I cradled Mirabai in my left arm comfortably in a half-sitting position and placed a spoonful of the cereal a little way back on her tongue. She sucked and smacked her lips, the cereal disappeared, and her mouth opened waiting for the next spoonful. We repeated this procedure until the whole 1½ tablespoonsful were gone. Obviously cereal made a pleasant change for my little one.

The best time to introduce solid or semisolid foods is usually somewhere between four and six months when several important growth factors exist: breast milk or formula alone is inadequate to support baby's normal growth, iron which has been stored in the body becomes depleted, the enzyme necessary to digest foods is present, and

*the infant's swallowing and chewing reflexes are sufficiently devel-
oped.*

*Learning to eat from a spoon is a very important experience. It
may seem temporarily easier to feed semisolids from a bottle with a
large-hole nipple, but you will only be delaying your baby's development in feeding. Use a slim baby spoon with no sharp edges. Place
a spoonful of food toward the back of the tongue, close to the roof of
the mouth, and let the baby do the rest. Rice cereal is good to start
with as it is easily digested.*

Mirabai has been getting rice cereal for four days now, so today
we are going to try barley. I am still using prepared baby cereal,
fortified with iron. I have increased the amount to 2 tablespoonsful
because her appetite is so good, and there were no ill effects (such
as diarrhea, gas, or rashes) from the rice cereal. And she is getting
more adept at getting it off the spoon now.

An aunt in Norway has sent Mirabai a little silver cup, and we
are going to try a little apple juice from the cup for the first time.
When I offer her the cup, she bites on the rim, and when I tilt it a
little, she seems surprised at the cool sweet liquid coming from it.
She lowers her head toward the cup again, wanting more.

*Rice cereal is the easiest of all cereals for babies to digest, but it
is also the lowest in protein. Introducing other varieties, such as oat
and barley, is good nutritionally, as well as getting baby used to
different flavors. However, I don't recommend buying the cereals that
are premixed with fruit (such as banana). These products have too
much sugar and other sweeteners in them, and it would be better to
use fresh mashed banana or other cooked mashed fruits.*

*Many dentists feel that as soon as an infant's teeth start coming
through, juices should be given only from a cup, as this helps prevent
cavities that could develop if a bottle is used. (Fruit juices lose their
vitamin content if they are heated and should be given at room temperature.) There are several kinds of baby cups. Some have lids with
drinking spouts, which are certainly less messy if baby grabs the cup
and tilts it. Others have heavy round bases to prevent tipping easily.*

*It is an individual preference for you and your baby, but you should
keep in mind that the cup should be unbreakable and have no sharp
edges.*

*Between twenty-eight and thirty-two weeks, babies demonstrate the
beginning of chewing patterns (up-and-down movements of the jaw);
and the tongue shows more maturity during spoon-feeding. The baby
can suck from a cup, but liquid often dribbles from the corners of his
mouth as he projects his tongue before swallowing.*

*Barley: Barley contains extremely small amounts of sodium (salt)
and is therefore good in a low-salt diet. Nutritionally, ¼ cup of
cooked barley provides approximately 46 calories, most coming from
carbohydrates. It does contain some protein, as well as thiamine,
niacin, and iron. Barley is one of the oldest foods known. Wild barley
was a dietary staple during some of the earliest civilizations, when a
paste was made from coarse barley flour. It was then eaten fresh or
dried for later use.*

Late September (6½ Months)

Mirabai is sleeping now from seven or eight o'clock at night to
around six A.M. or so, which is wonderful for us. It wasn't difficult,
although we had to let her cry for three nights. The first night she
cried strongly for about five minutes. The second night she was less
vehement, and by the third night a little whimper was all we heard.
And that was it. Before I put her to bed, we sit in the rocking chair
and I sing lullabies while she nurses. As soon as she wakes up
in the morning, I bring her into our bed and nurse her before we
get up.

*Some parents feel that starting solids will encourage their baby to
sleep through the night. Because of this belief, some infants are started
on solids as early as two months of age. Besides being inadvisable
nutritionally to start solids earlier than the fifth or sixth month, research has shown that feeding solids has no apparent effect on the
sleeping patterns of infants.*

Early October (6½ Months)

Mirabai is now well adjusted to all the cereals and seems to look forward to her "solid meals." She also gets an egg yolk with her breakfast cereal. She doesn't care for it hard-boiled but readily accepts it soft-boiled. She eats the yolk, and I finish the white.

Today I mashed ¼ ripe banana and added it to the breakfast menu. She loved it and finished every last bit, smacking her lips and smiling. Her two bottom teeth are through and the top ones are on their way.

It is recommended that your baby be given hard-boiled egg yolk initially, as it is easier to digest. However, if he seems to prefer a soft-cooked yolk and seems to tolerate it well, you might try offering it that way. You should watch for reactions, however. It is wise to withhold giving the white of egg until the child is twelve months of age, since it may cause an allergic reaction. If your child has no tendency toward allergies, and there are none in your family, it should be all right to give him a whole scrambled egg, or to use a whole egg in cooking, during the latter part of the first year.

Although not as inexpensive as they used to be, bananas are still affordable and available year round. This fruit is rich in natural fiber, high in potassium, low in sodium, and contains some vitamins A, C, and B_6 as well as thiamine, riboflavin, and niacin. Maybe out of a misconception that it is cheaper, easier, or faster to buy baby foods than make their own, many mothers will buy jars of mashed bananas. Because water is the first ingredient listed, the banana may well account for less than half of the jar's contents. Always review the labels on commercial baby foods. Ingredient information is shown in order of quantity of each ingredient. For example, the label on a jar of one manufacturer's strained bananas lists the following ingredients: water, fully ripened bananas, orange juice, sugar, tapioca starch modified, vitamin C, and citric acid. With respect to tapioca, I should mention that it is a complex starch, often difficult for an infant to digest. Most commercially prepared fruits, such as plums, bananas, and apricots, contain tapioca. It is cheaper and just as easy to mash a ripe banana, and it is certainly healthier for the baby.

Mid-October (7 Months)

I ran out of Mirabai's precooked cereal, so I made some regular oatmeal, which I gave her unsweetened with whole milk. She was hungry enough to eat half a bowlful, but certainly didn't like it as much as her baby cereal. She also had a soft-boiled egg yolk and a ½ cup of apple juice with vitamin C, which she really enjoyed.

It has been suggested that parents feed their infant hot cereals fortified with iron until the child is eighteen months old. Egg yolk and infant cereals fortified with iron are good sources of this important mineral, as is regular oatmeal. The vitamin C in apple juice will help the body absorb iron.

Note: Some infant formulas are also fortified with iron, as are most infant multiple vitamins. Since some experts feel there is a danger of iron toxicity, check with your pediatrician to ensure that your baby is receiving an adequate but not excessive amount of iron.

Late October (7½ Months)

Mirabai seems to be gaining too much weight. She is not crawling yet, and until six weeks ago was nursing every four to five hours around the clock as well as getting three meals a day. Bob takes care of her on Saturdays and Sundays while I am working and I think he tends to overfeed her. He likes to snack through the day and shares whatever he eats with Mirabai. I will write breakfast, lunch, and dinner menus for him and discourage him from giving her snacks in between. Now that she is getting an adequate supply of calories, protein, fat, and carbohydrates through her daily meals, I will cut down on breast-feeding, too.

Overfeeding can be a problem in infancy. The average healthy baby from five months to one year requires 47 calories per pound of weight. (These values are given as a basic guide. Degree of activity, sleeping patterns, and the general nature of the child must be taken into consideration.) If a baby weighs 17 pounds, he should take in approximately 800 calories a day. Most formulas contain around 20 calories per ounce, breast milk containing only a fraction less. If no solids are being given, this means that a baby needs five 8-ounce feedings a day (40 ounces).

If an infant is receiving three meals a day (approximating the following meal schedule), he will have a calorie intake of 320, which leaves 480 calories for bottle or breast milk, or approximately three feedings (24 ounces). Therefore, the amount of formula or nursing should now be cut back two feedings (16 ounces).

Meal Schedule

Breakfast:	¼ cup cooked cereal		*26 cal*
	1 egg yolk		*60 cal*
	½ small banana		*40 cal*
		Total	*126 cal*
Lunch:	1 tbsp. cottage cheese		*15 cal*
	1 tbsp. cooked carrots		*3 cal*
	1 breadstick		*38 cal*
	3 oz. grape juice		*60 cal*
		Total	*116 cal*
Dinner:	¼ cup mashed potato		*34 cal*
	1 tbsp. green beans		*3 cal*
	½ oz. hamburger		*41 cal*
		Total	*78 cal*

Total daily intake = 320 calories solids

Early November (7½ Months)

Lunch today consisted of 2 tablespoons of spinach, 1 tablespoon of yogurt with ¼ mashed banana, and juice. I made fresh pineapple and carrot juices in the juicer and mixed a little of each in a cup for Mirabai. She took a couple of sips and then turned her head away. After being offered the rest on a spoon, she finished it off and still had a little room for some rice pudding with raisins and milk.

Following her afternoon nap, we went into the garden to enjoy the sun. It was warm but not really hot, so I took off Mirabai's clothes and watched her play with the cat and some leaves while wearing just her sun hat.

Vitamin D can be produced by the body through the action of direct sunlight on the skin. If the body is not exposed to sufficient sunlight, a dietary source of vitamin D is necessary. The best source is fish liver oils, although children often find these unpalatable. An excellent alternative source is milk fortified with vitamin D.

Second Week of November (7½ Months)

My poor little one has intestinal flu, which started two nights ago with vomiting and a fever of 103°, followed by diarrhea. Yesterday the fever and vomiting had completely passed, thank heaven. I cut out most solids and have been primarily nursing Mirabai, although she ate a little rice cereal, which has a binding quality.

Today she had a loose but not liquid bowel movement; but her appetite has not returned, although she ate a little banana with plain yogurt. Later on I tried some mashed avocado but she refused it. Otherwise, she has been active and seems quite happy.

(After a week, her appetite was back to normal and she was on her regular solid foods schedule.)

When your child is sick, call your pediatrician regarding treatment, or take the baby for an examination, a diagnosis, and to find the possible cause of the illness. Babies' fevers tend to run quite high, and it is very important that they receive sufficient liquids to prevent dehydration, which could be very serious. At these times I would be flexible about giving your child bottles with juices, nighttime drinks, etc., and you could even go so far as allow Seven-Up, melted fruit gelatine, or any clear liquids your child will accept. If he won't take them in a cup, give them in a bottle. The most important thing is to make sure he is getting plenty of liquids. When your child is well again, you can revert to the rules of no juice in bottles, no bottles in bed, and no sodas.

When diarrhea is present, it is usually wise to stop all milk prod-

ucts, fruits (except for bananas), and most vegetables and meats. If your baby has a fever and no appetite, don't worry about giving him solids, but do make sure he is taking enough liquids.

There is some question as to whether one should continue nursing or giving formula when an infant has diarrhea. It would probably depend on the gravity of the illness, but I feel that in most mild cases one could continue to nurse. Some experts advocate giving strained carrots, diluted with an equal part of boiled water, as carrots are high in potassium and sodium; and rice and rice water may be helpful in controlling diarrhea.

Tea should not be given to babies. The xanthines in tea stimulate and excite infants and children and in some cases cause excessive urination. This in turn aggravates the fluid imbalance.

Late November (8 Months)

For Mirabai's lunch today I mashed half a banana and added it to a large tablespoonful of cottage cheese, a little of which she left on her plate. I have to be on guard not to insist that she finish everything—a temptation at times—and learn to recognize the first sign that tells me she has had enough. When her attention starts to wander, her mouth doesn't open wide, or she starts to play with her food, its time to take the bowl away. If I don't, the next signs aren't so subtle. She just whams the spoon down like an auctioneer with a gavel, and there it is, baby food everywhere.

There seems to be a universal parental attitude, probably passed down through generations, that dinner isn't finished until the plate is empty. Waste is sinful. This may be true, but how can we gauge an infant's appetite? A little baby cannot tell us how hungry he is, what he enjoys eating, or when he is full. So we tend to use our own concepts of how much he needs, believing he should be full when his plate is empty. This can be when the miserable habit of overeating starts. Children have fine appetite control and react immediately when their stomachs send the message that they are full. This is very valuable in learning just how much food the body needs, and I wonder how many adults are still so well attuned.

Because your baby cannot talk, he will relay his feelings through various kinds of sign language. Each child has his own way of communicating, and parents must learn to observe the signs and respond to his needs.

Late November (8½ Months)

I have been flat on my back with the flu and a very high fever, and have been too sick to care about anything or anyone, including Mirabai. Fortunately, I have a good support system in my husband, Bob, and our two teenage sons. They have taken care of Mirabai and fed her well, and she doesn't seem to be suffering. In spite of my inability to give her any attention, and the fact that I had to stop breast-feeding abruptly, she is her usual happy self. As I had been taking lots of aspirin for the fever and was only taking liquids, I refrained from nursing her. Luckily, my breasts did not become engorged. Instead of my nursing Mirabai first thing in the morning, Bob would warm some formula when she woke up, put her in my arms, and, holding her close, I would give her the bottle. She seemed perfectly content. Although now I am well again, Mirabai has not nursed for five days, so this seems to be an appropriate time to stop. She is almost eight and a half months old, is a good weight, and the weaning did not seem to cause any trauma. Ten day later, while I was doing exercises without a bra, Mirabai started playing with my nipple. She didn't try to put it in her mouth and I knew then that she did not miss nursing and had been ready for weaning.

The time for weaning a baby is a personal choice and different circumstances may influence one's decision. Some mothers may have to return to work and would find it inconvenient to continue nursing. Others may express milk for daytime feedings and nurse only mornings and evenings.

Medical opinion is overwhelmingly in favor of breast-feeding, as it is nutritionally and psychologically better for babies. Apparently, the longer an infant can nurse, the better. However, the day will come when you have to decide to stop nursing, and a couple of factors should be kept in mind. During the nine- to twelve-month period, an infant's desire to explore his environment begins to exceed his hunger for food. His interest in bottle or breast is decreasing as the discovery of his increased motor activity becomes more important to him. This time, then, seems developmentally conducive to weaning. Solid-food eating habits also often improve after weaning because the infant is not so easily satiated by liquids.

Until the tenth to twelfth month, the average infant has relied mostly on sucking and swallowing to take his food. The ability to chew then swallow firmer foods has been progressively maturing, however, so ideally around twelve months seems like a good time to stop nursing. This would also be the time to start weaning your child from the bottle. Prolonged bottle feeding may cause two health problems. One is the bottle-mouth syndrome when severe dental cavities are caused by bed- and naptime bottles. The other is iron-deficiency anemia, caused by drinking an excessive amount of cow's milk, which contains negligible amounts of iron. (Parents concerned that thumb-sucking may be substituted for bottle feedings will be comforted to know that, as a rule, a baby that has not started thumb-sucking by eight months will generally not develop the habit thereafter.)

From about twelve to fifteen months of age, a toddler can hold and drink from a cup independently and should be able to take all his liquids this way.

One last observation on breast-feeding, which is very subjective and has not been substantiated scientifically. The hesitation of a mother to stop nursing after the first year may have more to do with the mother's psychological attachment to it than to the child's needs. There is tremendous comfort, warmth, peace, and joy in the intimacy of nursing, and often a sense of "emptiness," as well as relief, follows when breast-feeding is discontinued.

Early December (8½ Months)

Mirabai has eight teeth now (although no molars as yet) and her gag reflex is well developed. She grasps things with her hands but doesn't use her thumb and index finger yet.

I decided to try finger foods for lunch today. We started with a stoned-wheat cracker and cream cheese, which she seemed to enjoy squishing in her tiny fingers. It must have tasted good, too, for the whole thing disappeared in no time. We followed this with a little meat cake, a few pieces of cooked carrot, and a slice of peeled ripe pear, all of which were accompanied by appreciative noises. The floor was a disaster, as was the high chair, but it took no time to clean up and when naptime came along, it was a very contented little Mirabai who went right off to sleep.

Indications that an infant is ready for finger foods are his ability to sit up, grasp and bring an object to his mouth, and basic up-and-down chewing movements of the jaw. Initially babies grasp things with the palm of the hand, so the size and shape of finger foods are important. Start out giving him a piece of dry toast or a cracker. Once the pincer reflex is developed, the variety of finger foods offered can be increased, as your baby will be able to pick up small pieces of cooked vegetables, meat, cheese, or fruit with his thumb and index finger.

Mid-December (9 Months)

My little one's eating habits are changing and her rejection of certain foods shows her dislikes very clearly. Avocado is the most recent offender. I have tried it in combination with cottage cheese, beans, and bananas, all of which she loves, but she recognizes the avocado in all of them. The look of loathing and disgust she displays as she spits it out has made me give up this delicious fruit for the time being.

Avocado is extremely nutritious, containing at least eight essential vitamins and five vital minerals. It is high in vitamin A (carotene), folic acid, vitamin C, iron, vitamin E, and magnesium. It is an excellent source of potassium and also contains riboflavin, thiamine, pyridoxine, pantothenic acid, niacin, and choline. Its smooth texture, gentle flavor, and easy digestibility make it a desirable food for infants. Knowing this, I tried every conceivable way to serve it to Mirabai, but for now all is in vain.

When a child exhibits a strong dislike for certain foods, this should be accepted. Foods with the same nutritional values can be substituted, although it may take several other kinds to compensate for the nutrients of the one food the baby rejects. With a little knowledge and some imagination, however, both mother and baby can win. If the rejected food is taken away and not offered again for some months, the infant's tastes may change and he may later accept it.

Variety is important to an adequate diet and a mother's challenge with a new baby is to introduce him to a large selection of nutritious foods. Problems will arise if the parents are fussy eaters. If Father won't eat certain foods, Mother usually goes out of her way not to prepare them for the rest of the family. In the same way, Mother seldom buys produce that she dislikes. In this way, rejection of many foods may be passed down from parents to children. Having a new baby around should encourage all the members of the family to examine their own eating habits.

When introducing a new food, start with a very tiny portion. The child may look at it, feel it, or just smell it initially. This is part of learning to accept it. Some children reject all foods of a certain texture, so it may help to combine a soft food with a crisp or chewy food. The color and attractiveness of food influence appetites as well. Fresh steamed broccoli, for instance, is bright green. If overcooked and left standing around, it becomes soggy and a murky green. The same is true of fresh spinach. Mix the colors of vegetables to make them more appealing; for instance, combine small pieces of cauliflower, carrots, yellow squash, and green vegetables to stimulate an unenthusiastic palate. Do not verbally reinforce your child's dislike of a food. Psychologically he may resist trying it again at a later time, even if he would like to try it.

Late December (9½ Months)

For the first time, Mirabai joined the whole family for our evening meal. I had made *får-i-kål*, a delicious Norwegian lamb and cabbage dish, which I served with potatoes boiled in their skins. Mirabai shared everything from my plate, chopped up, of course, and loved it all.

Eating together as a family group builds closeness and family solidarity. Increasingly, however, families tend not to eat together as often as they did in the past. We are becoming a society of "snackers," often eating hurriedly and alone while engaged in other activities. Sharing meals in a warm, cheerful environment can evoke in all of us positive reactions toward specific foods that go far beyond their nutritional values.

Mid-January (10 Months)

I don't know if it is her age, the irregular routine caused by our Christmas celebrations, or because she is cutting teeth—her lower lateral incisors—but Mirabai's appetite has decreased, and for the first time since she was born, she has a diaper rash. I am giving her food she is familiar with and likes, but still she takes only a few spoonfuls before spitting it out. It is frustrating and a little disconcerting, but as she sleeps soundly, has rosy cheeks, is very lively, and still seems to be gaining weight, she must be getting sufficient nutrients.

Changes in daily routine, teething, and biochemical conditions in the body that influence the acceptance of food may be among the many reasons a child's appetite decreases. Parents often worry unduly about this. If your infant is off his food but gaining weight, is active, and is sleeping well, try to relax. Children are extremely sensitive to negative as well as positive emotions, and will react to your anxiety. If no fuss is made over these periods of poor eating, the problem will resolve itself. However, if your child appears listless, loses weight, or continues to reject food for some time, you should consult your doctor. A healthy child will eat when he is hungry. If he doesn't want his meal, remove it. Don't offer alternative foods, coax, play, or use tricks to make him eat. And remember that babies' stomachs are small. One tablespoonful of each food group for each of his three meals will give adequate nutrition to a twelve-month-old.

Late January (10½ Months)

I may have found a solution to Mirabai's poor eating habits. Instead of feeding her at her normal times of eight A.M., noon, and five P.M., I wait until she seems hungry. It certainly worked last night. I warmed up some leftover lamb, cabbage, potatoes, and carrots at 6:30 P.M., and she ate a huge bowlful. This was followed by some fruit gelatine. Instead of feeding her breakfast with Bob and me at eight A.M. this morning, I waited a while. Then I gave her some natural baby food cereal that came from the health-food store, followed by a soft-boiled egg, and a cup of orange juice with ¼ teaspoon brewer's yeast. Again, she ate everything readily.

It is important to remember that changes can occur in a child's eating patterns. Eating should be a pleasure as well as a necessity. Most of us don't enjoy eating if we have no appetite, especially if forced to eat. It takes keen observation and good intuition to recognize when your child is hungry and needs to eat, as opposed to waiting until he is very hungry before feeding him. Also some experts feel that "starving a child to eat" will not promote good eating patterns.

Children are normally rhythmic in their habits, so satisfying their hunger should be in tune with that rhythm. Therefore, meals should be served at the same time each day whenever possible. This may conflict with adult schedules initially, but eventually infants seem to adapt to the rest of the family's mealtimes, probably because they enjoy the social interaction.

Fatigue is often a major factor in loss of appetite. An exhausted child's appetite is seldom restored until he has had a nap or a good night's sleep.

I found brewer's yeast to be an effective appetite stimulant for Mirabai, and it is an excellent source of protein and the natural B-complex vitamins. However, her pediatrician recommended only ⅛ teaspoon initially, increasing the amount slowly over several months to 1 teaspoon. If you wish to start your baby on brewer's yeast, you should talk to your doctor first.

Mid-February (11 Months)

Most of America is freezing right now while here the sun is shining and it is warm and beautiful. Mirabai and I picked camellias and iris from the garden, listened to the birds singing, and enjoyed the smell of freshly cut grass. After such a lovely time, we were more than ready for lunch. As our finances and budget have been feeling the effects of the economy, I have been using my imagination and trying to create tasty meals based on beans, rice, or pasta. I had already cooked rice and lima beans, which I reheated for lunch, with some freshly steamed broccoli. I gave Mirabai a tablespoonful of each, turned on Mahler's First Symphony, which has lots of boom-boom, and watched the rice and vegetables disappear with much banging-of-the-spoon accompaniment and laughter. Mirabai wasn't at all concerned that she was eating variations of the same foods for the second or third day. Banana with milk finished off her lunch, giving her everything she needed for a balanced meal. Before putting her down for her nap, I gave her a warm bath and a gentle massage with baby oil.

Lima beans are incomplete in protein, but combined with rice they make a complete protein, including all the essential eight amino acids. Broccoli provides a substantial amount of vitamins A and C, in addition to some calcium, iron, thiamine, riboflavin, and niacin. The banana provides more of the same, plus potassium; and milk contains calcium, protein, and vitamins A and D.

Nutritious foods do not have to be expensive. For instance, the protein in meat or fish can be substituted by the protein in beans and rice, which can be prepared in a variety of healthy and delicious ways. Vegetables and fruits that are plentiful and in season are the most economical to use along with bananas, which are available year-round and are inexpensive for the nutritional value they provide. It is also possible to keep the food budget down by utilizing cheaper cuts of meat and poultry for soups and stews, using lots of fresh vegetables, and combining incomplete proteins as shown in the table on page 29.

PERCENTILE STANDARDS FOR GROWTH
BOYS (BIRTH TO 24 MOS)
Adapted from NCHS Growth Charts, 1976

PERCENTILE STANDARDS FOR GROWTH
GIRLS (BIRTH TO 24 MOS)
Adapted from NCHS Growth Charts, 1976

Reproduced by permission from, Pediatric Nutrition Handbook.
Copyright American Academy of Pediatrics 1979.

Many other things can give us a feeling of well-being and are absolutely free: sunshine, a tree, beautiful flower, music, or a little body massage. Children are extremely sensitive to parental emotions and moods, and if you are anxious, your child will be affected. With a little conscious effort, it should be possible to turn this mood around and make your little one's mealtimes happy and free from stress, and allow him to enjoy his food.

Mid-March (1 Year)

Mirabai and I visited the pediatrician today for a first-year checkup. She is shy with strangers and became very upset when the nurse tried to put her on the scales to check her height and weight. Whether the measurements were totally accurate is questionable, but they were probably close enough. After her initial "torturous" experience, Mirabai accepted the rest of the examination with a little more composure, and she received a clean bill of health at a weight of 22 pounds and a height of 28½ inches.

At six months of age, the average infant will have doubled his birth weight. By his first birthday, as the child enters the toddler phase, he will have reached approximately three times his birth weight, stand about 29 inches tall, and have six teeth. (See the following charts for a breakdown of the first two years' growth rates.)

An annual assessment of a child's weight and height gives important indicators of normal growth, as does measuring the head circumference. The most critical and rapid period of human brain growth begins at conception and continues into the second year. Brain cells increase in number until the child is twelve to fifteen months of age, and they increase thereafter in mass and size. A rapid growth in brain mass is accompanied by an increased head circumference. Malnourished children usually have smaller head circumferences than those of their well-nourished peers. These children have also been reported to perform more poorly on intelligence tests than do well-nourished children. It seems that a malnourished infant has less chance of recovering intellectual defects caused by serious nutritional defi-

ciencies than those who become malnourished later in life. A child's ability to catch up also appears to be influenced by the length of the period of deprivation. Research has also shown that children who have been malnourished for no more than four months are less handicapped than those who have been deprived for longer periods of time.

Late March (12½ Months)

Now that Mirabai is a year old, I see a lot of changes in her. She is strong-willed and is developing a distinct personality. She insists on feeding herself and has become very opinionated about what she will eat. If what she is being served doesn't please her, even without so much as a taste, she turns ninety degrees in her high chair, shakes her head vigorously, and clamps her mouth shut. And there is no consistency to this young lady's likes and dislikes. She may accept something today that she refused yesterday and may refuse again tomorrow. While she wants to use a spoon, it is purely accidental and quite miraculous if she scoops up any food, as she plunges the spoon into her bowl impatiently and usually turns it upside down before it reaches her mouth. Most of a meal ends up outside her body, on the floor, and covering the high chair. If she is very hungry, I am allowed to guide her hand with the spoon, and we might get a couple of spoonsful of food into her mouth. Otherwise, it's back to finger feeding.

This is a very trying time indeed. It calls for tremendous patience and understanding, but it is important not to discourage this independence. Self-feeding is one of a child's first steps toward independence and controlling his environment. The learning process can be frustrating at this age because motor skills are not sufficiently developed, so a mother's role becomes that of teacher. Show your child how to hold a spoon, gently bringing his hand to his mouth, and he will eventually get the necessary movements under control. It can be a long, slow process, since children tend to fluctuate between resistance and cooperation, but your efforts will be rewarded when your toddler shows you "I can do it all by myself."

Lastly, as left- or right-handed dominance has not been estab-lished and should not be enforced, allow your child to grab the spoon with either hand. In another three or four months, finer control of the wrist and fingers will be established and self-feeding will be consid-erably more efficient and speedy.

Early April (12½ Months)

I occasionally give Mirabai a dried apricot for a snack or treat. Since she has no molars, she mostly gums the fruit, working on it for quite a while. She takes it out of her mouth, examines it, pops it back in, and generally seems to enjoy the taste and experience. However, the apricot comes out whole in her bowel movements as do whole corn kernels. Obviously she is not able to chew them up. Fortunately, Mirabai has never choked on food. I am very careful to mash or finely cut her food because even though she has a few teeth, she doesn't seem to take the time to chew her food.

The problem of toddlers and small children choking on food has become alarming enough for the federal government to appoint a national task force to study the problem. Although the study is in-complete at the time of this writing, results from 41 states show that over a period of 3 years, 276 children have died from choking on food, with hot dogs and grapes being the biggest offenders. Always keep in mind that toddlers and small children often do not chew food thoroughly, so consider not giving them potential choke foods until they are older.

Some potential choke foods are peanuts and other nuts, whole corn, grapes, cherries, whole orange segments (with membranes), raw whole carrots, and hot dogs.

Mid-April (13 Months)

For lunch today I steamed a caulifloweret, cut half a carrot into small pieces, and reheated some leftover green peas and liver. When arranged in the baby dish, the food looked very attractive. Mirabai was hungry and studied her food with great interest. She took the spoon in one hand, but used the other to pick up the vegetables. She then carefully picked up a piece of liver and put it in her mouth, but quickly spat it out. Her older brother, William, was eating the same food and showed her how much he liked it, saying, "Mirabai, this is so good." She watched him and ate a little more of the liver, but most of it ended up on the floor.

In addition to being one of the more reasonably priced meats, liver has many other attributes. It is easy to prepare and quick to cook. It is also one of the best sources of iron, vitamins A and B, and minerals, and contains about the same amount of calories as chicken or turkey. Its one drawback is that it is high in cholesterol, although this should not adversely affect a healthy baby.

Calf's liver has the smoothest texture and is very tender if not overcooked. Beef liver is not so tender, and pork liver contains more connective tissue than beef or calf's liver as well as having a stronger and slightly bitter flavor.

To prepare liver, it should be washed as little as possible to avoid removing valuable vitamins and minerals, and it should not be soaked, scalded, or cooked at high temperatures. Liver from young animals requires only brief cooking—just enough to heat the meat through and change its color. Long cooking or high temperatures will make it tough and dry. Pat liver pieces dry with a paper towel, dredge them lightly in flour, and sauté briefly in a little vegetable oil until brown, turning once to cook both sides. Liver can also be broiled (brush meat with a little oil and lemon juice), baked, and even made into meat loaf. (See Index for recipes.) Whatever way you prepare liver, the flavor is distinctive and it may take your child a while to develop a taste for it. It is worth persevering until you find the method of preparation that makes the dish most appealing to him.

Parents and siblings are models that younger children emulate, especially in eating and behavior patterns. It is thought that older siblings actually exert an even greater influence than parents in these areas.

Late April (13½ Months)

Last week for dinner I gave Mirabai mashed potatoes and carrots, followed by cottage cheese and cantaloupe, and she ate it all. When I tried the same foods today, she wouldn't touch them. I am concerned that if I try to coax her with alternative foods I may be encouraging finicky eating habits. Her two teenage brothers, who believe they are authorities on child-rearing because they have just outgrown childhood themselves, knew exactly what to do and shared such wisdom as "If she doesn't want it, take the food away," and "Don't give her anything else to eat until she finishes what she has." Then they watch while, with an uneasy mind, I pick Mirabai up and put her to bed without any dinner.

I do believe in consistency and discipline, but it is sometimes difficult to follow through and I wonder if I am doing the right thing. The boys' absolute assurance on the subject annoys me, and I point out to William his problem with eating beans and many vegetables. He quickly answers that that is exactly the point; he doesn't want us to make the same mistakes with Mirabai that were made with him! This is a subject continually being raised by both boys, who feel we should have been more strict and consistent with them. Mirabai has always received a lot of attention, but if she cries for something she can't have, she is totally ignored, and she has never thrown a tantrum because she wasn't allowed a cookie, candy, or toy that caught her fancy. She may cry out of frustration for a while, then everything is fine again. Persistent angry tears have never given her good results, and this makes everyone's life much easier.

Discipline is a very important part of a child's life and is necessary in establishing good eating habits. However, it is not always easy to enforce, especially when one is anxious that a child has not had enough to eat. We are vulnerable and open to manipulation, and children are remarkably astute at using this advantage. It is important to be consistent without being authoritarian, stubborn, punitive, or angry.

Early May (13½ Months)

Mirabai is having regular oatmeal with milk for breakfast. She has a spoon and I am sitting watching her. Although the spoon is used only occasionally, she is eating happily and enjoys seeing the oatmeal squeeze through her little fingers when she makes a fist. There is oatmeal splattered on the walls, and the floor and high chair are covered. Mirabai is having a wonderful time. I am not. It is difficult to watch her, and I want to take the bowl and spoon and feed her myself—neat, clean, and easy. She will not learn to feed herself if I do, but at what point should I intervene? It is important and natural for toddlers to touch food. Using fingers is acceptable for certain foods, and a toddler is not yet able to distinguish between those that may be handled and those that may not, and why. Nor does neatness count. However, this is the time to start learning. I don't want Mirabai to think she is bad, dirty, or naughty because she is touching her food or making a mess, but when she loses interest in using the spoon altogether, I take it from her and feed her myself. If she refuses to give up her spoon, I get another one and use that. When she is full, I remove the bowl immediately so that leftovers can't be used as playthings.

One day I gave Mirabai her spoon and some yogurt in a bowl. Apparently she couldn't eat it fast enough with a spoon, and fingers were of no use, so before I realized what was happening, she picked up the bowl and had yogurt trickling down her face, dress, chair, and the floor. It was a terrible mess but I had to laugh.

Parents should understand that children in this age group need some freedom to experiment in order to assert independence. If a toddler is to master new skills, he must have adult approval of his trials-and-errors in learning.

"Shaping" and "fading" are two techniques professionals use to teach self-feeding. Shaping is the reinforcement of each step needed for the task to be learned. The first step is taught, then reinforced, and when it is learned, the next step is added and reinforced. This

*pattern continues until the desired behavior is obtained. An example
of teaching spoon feeding by shaping works in the following way:*

Step 1: Child looks at spoon.

Step 2: Child moves hand toward spoon.

Step 3: Child touches spoon.

Step 4: Child picks up spoon.

Step 5: Child puts spoon in dish.

Step 6: Child scoops up food.

Step 7: Child brings food to mouth.

Step 8: Child takes food off spoon.

Step 9: Child returns spoon to dish.
Reinforcement = Bites of food or praise as each step is accomplished.

*Fading offers a different approach. Instead of requiring the child
to proceed through several steps, the trainer's cues are changed as
the child's skills develop. For example, the trainer holds the child's
hand around a spoon and puts him through the motions of scooping
food into it, bringing the spoon to his mouth, and returning the spoon
to the dish. As the child gradually assumes independent movement,
physical assistance is decreased, and the trainer provides help only
when needed to complete the task.*

*Most parents use these techniques instinctively in teaching their
children self-feeding, but the psychological definitions of shaping and
fading may clarify the steps and help parents work through this difficult stage more easily.**

*Source: Nutrition in Infancy and Childhood, Peggy L. Pipes, The C. V. Mosby Company, St. Louis, Mo., 1977.

Mid-May (14 Months)

The skies have been overcast for weeks, but today there is a gentle breeze, the sun is shining and at last it feels like summer. After Mirabai's morning nap, we decided to have a picnic lunch in the garden. Mirabai ran around dressed only in a little sun hat while I spread a blanket under the apricot tree and brought out a tray with wheat crackers, Swiss cheese, and grape juice for us. After enjoying this light but satisfying lunch, Mirabai played with the cat while I wrote a letter. Although I hadn't intended to stay outside too long, two hours passed in a wink and I decided to give Mirabai a cooling bath. After some bathtub play and a little baby-oil massage, we snacked on some leftover white beans, cottage cheese, and watermelon. Mirabai fed herself, getting almost as many beans on herself and the floor as in her tummy, which made me realize I should have waited for the bath. But she is trying hard to use the spoon and is learning. If I were a little braver and let her eat everything independently, she would probably become adept very quickly.

In warmer weather it is wise to serve lighter meals, with a greater emphasis on fruits and cheese, foods that don't require cooking and are nutritious, refreshing, and easily digested.

Cheese is a concentrated source of many of the nutrients found in milk. It is an excellent source of protein and calcium, contributes significant amounts of phosphorus and riboflavin to the diet, and contains vitamin B_{12} and magnesium. Its high-quality protein, vitamins, and minerals make it a very valuable food. Milk and dairy products are the richest source of calcium in the North American diet, and the recommended daily requirement is 800 milligrams for a one- to three-year-old child.

Mozzarella, jack, Swiss (Jarlsberg), cheddar, or Bel Paese cheeses are good to use for finger foods. Parmesan cheese has a strong flavor but is very rich in protein, so let your child eat it if he likes it. All types of cottage cheese are good and blend well with fruits. Ricotta is a creamy Italian cheese used mostly in cooking, but it can be served with fruit as well. It has a higher fat content than cottage cheese and is an excellent source of calcium.

Another benefit from cheese has recently been found. Charles Schachtele, an oral microbiologist, made some interesting discoveries when measuring the impact of cheese on teeth. Swiss, jack, and aged cheddar cheeses were found to be very effective in blocking formation of the acid that can cause tooth decay. Blue, Brie, Gouda, and mozzarella cheeses are not as effective, but they still inhibit tooth decay. The least effective cheeses in retarding acid buildup are feta, provolone, cream cheese, and all processed cheeses.

Toddlers need to be encouraged to feed themselves, progressing from finger foods to utensils. Eating is a sensual experience for a young child and one must expect messiness in self-feeding. Parents should be encouraged to allow the child to develop independence in this as soon as he is ready.

Late May (14½ Months)

We had Chinese food for dinner last night. I stir-fried some boned cut-up chicken in the wok with bean sprouts, mushrooms, onions, and snow peas, and served them with basmati rice. Mirabai ate very little, as she had had a late lunch and was obviously not very hungry. I should have taken her cue. She has well-regulated eating habits, does not eat for the sake of it, and I never force food on her. However, we were having strawberries and kiwi fruit for dessert, which she loves, so I gave her some. The colors of the fruit appealed to her and she stuffed them into her mouth as fast as she could, with obvious pleasure. Later that night everything came back up, poor little one. But I needn't have worried, for when she woke up this morning, she was chirpy as ever and ready for breakfast.

Recently Mirabai threw back her head to laugh and I noticed that two upper molars had broken through. Besides a slight decline in appetite, some drooling, and putting her fingers in her mouth, she showed no problems. I had worried that she would have a difficult time cutting the molars, as her gums were so swollen and looked painful, but obviously they didn't bother her.

The time when teeth are cut varies greatly from child to child. The following schedule gives the approximate time deciduous teeth (baby teeth) should show through:

- Lower central incisors (2): 5–9 months
- Upper central incisors (2): 8–12 months
- Upper lateral incisors (2): 10–12 months
- Lower lateral incisors (2): 12–15 months
- First molars (4): 10–16 months
- Canines (4): 16–20 months
- Second molars (4): 20–30 months

The average child will have six teeth at one year of age, twelve teeth at eighteen months, sixteen teeth at two years, and twenty teeth at two and a half years.

Although all children's reactions differ, teething will present problems and changes in their daily lives to some degree. Doctors feel that teething does not cause fever, diarrhea, or a runny nose. However, these symptoms seem to appear with teething almost universally. A baby may develop diaper rash for the first time, be cranky and irritable, or suffer from loss of appetite. Since so many teeth are being cut during the first two years, there will be many trying times. On the positive side, children seem to bounce back remarkably quickly from whatever symptoms they had; a high fever and no appetite for several days may be all but forgotten within a week. If your child has a fever, check with your pediatrician first and give the child plenty of liquids. It is important to get the fever down as soon as possible. Should your baby have diarrhea, cut out fruits, milk, and milk products until the symptoms have disappeared. Plain boiled rice or rice water can be helpful in stopping diarrhea. Diaper rash should be kept to a minimum by changing your child as soon as he becomes wet or soiled. A mixture of Desitin and A & D Ointment makes a soothing skin barrier. Fresh air and a little sunshine also promote healing.

Teething is a troublesome time for parents as well as baby. Extra love, patience, attention, and cuddling are needed. Don't be concerned that your child will become a hypochondriac if you give him unlimited attention and love while he is feeling so bad. If you give him the love he needs when he is well, extra care during an illness will have no negative long-term effects. If times of illness are the only times a child gets special consideration, love, and attention, this may cause a future problem.

Mid-June (15 Months)

Mirabai and I went for a long walk today. I put her in the stroller and we went to the shopping mall, mainly to window-shop. We hadn't had lunch and were hungry, so I looked for a place to eat. A hot dog from the fast-food stand was outrageously expensive for a puny-looking wiener on a dry white bun. The hamburgers didn't look any better, so we went to the health-food store and bought some Bulgarian yogurt with raspberries in the bottom, a small carton of milk, and a peach, all of which Mirabai and I shared. We sat on a bench in the sun and watched the people pass by. Little sparrows came hopping up to us, looking for crumbs, so next time we come on this small adventure, we will bring some crackers or bread so Mirabai can feed the birds as well as herself.

Taking children shopping is usually a necessity, seldom a pleasure. Little ones get bored and restless very easily, and often by the time the parent decides to stop for a snack or lunch, they are too tired to eat. One of the most common reasons for poor appetite is fatigue, so it is wise not to wait too long before stopping for a break. Both mother and child will benefit in the long run.

Sitting in a chair for any length of time is very trying for a child, and there are usually alternatives to going to restaurants and coffee shops. If the weather is good, look for a park, a small grassy area, or even a bench, and have a minipicnic. Either bring food or buy what you need at the store. Cheese and crackers, fruit, and milk or juice will be plenty for a shopping luncheon. Occasionally, of course, the whole family may decide to go to a restaurant, and this requires a little more forethought. If your baby is very young and eating puréed or mashed foods, take a small food mill with you. Any vegetable, meat, or starch can be turned into baby food, but keep in mind that the restaurant food will probably contain quite a bit of salt (although I don't feel an occasional meal with salt will be harmful). As the baby grows older, he will be able to share the restaurant meal with you. The main concern is how to keep him entertained while you wait for dinner. A story, simple puzzle, or toy will keep a toddler occupied, but your attention and participation will be needed. Expecting a small child to entertain himself will probably not work.

Late June (15½ Months)

A few weeks ago I attended a cooking demonstration by Marion Cunningham (editor of *The Fannie Farmer Cookbook*). She made breads and a fresh fruit soup. Many fruit soups originated in Scandinavia and making this one in class brought back memories. My mother's recipe was made with blueberries picked from the mountain slopes by my father. She mixed the berries with water, sugar, and a little potato flour (to thicken). After bringing the mixture to a boil and cooking it for a few minutes, she would cool it and serve it for dessert with a dollop of whipped cream. Similar soups were made with apples, rhubarb, or rosehips, and oats, semolina, or rye would sometimes be added. It was a very nutritious dessert. Mrs. Cunningham's soup called for fresh strawberries, a little sugar, yogurt, a dash of Grand Marnier, and fresh mint, mixed well in the blender. It was delicious.

It has been very hot recently, so I thought it would be a pleasant dessert to try on my family, leaving out the Grand Marnier for Mirabai's sake, and using homemade yogurt. It tasted good, and I refrigerated it for several hours so that it would be well chilled. On opening the refrigerator to serve my new specialty, I was amazed to find only 4 tablespoonsful left. I gave what little there was to Bob and Mirabai, who loved it. The mystery of the disappearing fruit soup was cleared up when my eldest son, William, came home and complimented me on the great strawberry smoothie I had made! A couple of days later I tried again. This time everyone shared it and Mirabai ate a whole bowlful.

We are more familiar with hot soups, made with meat and vegetables, than with cold fruit soups. However, this is a truly delicious way of encouraging your family to eat yogurt and fresh fruit. Straw-berries are an excellent source of vitamin C, and yogurt makes a good substitute for a serving of milk.

Fourth of July (15½ Months)

It would have been nice to go to the beach on this hot Independence Day, but the freeways and beaches are so crowded that we are content to celebrate at home. A lot of friends and their children are coming over for a potluck party. One family is bringing potato salad, another a green salad, and someone else the buns and paper goods; and we are going to barbecue the traditional hot dogs and hamburgers and make homemade ice cream. The kids will have fresh lemonade using lemons from the garden, and the grown-ups can also have beer or wine.

The garden is full of laughter, talk, and the occasional scream of excitement from one of the little ones. The ice-cream machine is churning away, the barbecue has stopped smoking, and Bob is expertly cooking the meat and corn. Mirabai is in her element. She loves parties. Right now she is sitting under the apricot tree with Grandma, balancing a paper plate on her little knees and tasting all the different foods, while her little friend Robert is cleaning up everyone's plate, whether they have finished or not. Maybe the relaxed atmosphere, sunshine, and wonderful company have something to do with it, but everything we ate tasted so delicious, and now we are waiting for the grand finale, the homemade ice cream. There is nothing in the world so good as do-it-yourself ice cream, even if it is a little soft, and it disappears in no time. Everyone helps with the cleaning up, and as the sun is setting, the little ones are getting sleepy. Mirabai doesn't protest when I tuck her into bed. It has been a very special and happy day.

There are few foods as typically American—and enjoyed by so many people—as hot dogs and hamburgers. Recently, however, the nutritional value of the hot dog has come under attack. The ingredients listed on a typical pack of wieners read as follows: pork, water, beef, salt, corn syrup, dextrose, flavoring, sodium ascorbate, sodium nitrate. Which makes this food something to avoid serving to toddlers or children—or adults for that matter—on a regular basis. But sometimes the hot dog typifies a special occasion, such as the Fourth of July or a baseball game, and if the occasions are fairly infrequent, the sentimental value can override the nutritional one. I feel this also applies to cookies and candies, which should be allowed only on special occasions.

The following is an excerpt taken from a condensed Consumer Reports *article dated May 1980:*

"Hot dogs are not overly nutritious. They are cheap, but high in fat. The sodium content of those purchased by Consumer Reports *in 1979 varied from 228 mg to 850 mg per hot dog—with most of them containing about 400 mg. Like all cured meats they contain small amounts of nitrite or nitrate. Nitrite gives cured meat its characteristic flavor and color and inhibits the growth of bacteria, including the source of botulism, toxin. However, nitrite may combine with amines (natural compounds found in most foods) to form nitrosamines, which cause cancer in animals. The amounts of nitrites and nitrosamines in cured meats have been reduced in recent years, but nitrite is still added to foods because there is as yet no suitable substitute for it as an inhibitor of botulism. Some hot dogs are nitrite free and contain no preservatives. They must be kept frozen until cooked."**

Nitrosamines are also a normal by-product of the bacteria that live in the digestive tract. We appear to have learned to live with low levels of them. Researchers state that fiber lowers the concentration of nitrosamines by increasing the size and frequency of stools and speeding their elimination from the system. The message is to cut down on fats and meats in our diet, and increase fiber through eating fruits, whole grains, and vegetables.

*Copyright 1980 by Consumers Union of United States, Inc., Mount Vernon, N.Y. 10550. Excerpted by permission from *Consumer Reports*, May 1980.

Mid-July (16 Months)

I had an interesting conversation with a friend yesterday on the advantages and disadvantages of meat in babies' diets. She had read a book specifically mentioning the dangers of a vegetarian diet for babies and the possibility that this could cause deformities and deficiencies in bone structure. Such things could happen if an infant was kept on an extreme vegetarian diet excluding milk products and eggs, and if the parents lacked knowledge of how to combine incomplete proteins to make them complete.

I have mixed feelings about meat and realize I serve it much less frequently now than I did ten years ago. In the past there was a lot of controversy about livestock being injected with stilbestrol (a hormone to promote growth) and antibiotics, so I decided to call the U.S. Department of Agriculture to get the facts. I spoke with two meat inspectors, a supervisor, and a veterinarian who works with livestock. Each reassured me that stilbestrol has now been federally outlawed. All animals are vaccinated when young to prevent a variety of diseases, in much the same way that babies are vaccinated against human diseases. Also poultry are given antibiotics of which all traces should be gone by the time they are slaughtered. All meats and poultry are checked randomly, and if any contamination is found, that meat is not made available for public consumption. That was good to hear.

More and more Americans are reducing their intake of meat, sometimes for financial reasons, sometimes for their health. Although all processed meats, such as ham, bacon, sausage and luncheon meats, contain additives, increased consumer awareness has had a beneficial influence on the meat production industry.

If any kind of vegetarian diet is contemplated for an infant, it is extremely important that it be done with a complete understanding of how to provide total nutrition. It cannot be emphasized enough that one should not put babies on a vegetarian diet without first reading as much qualified literature as possible and becoming aware of the knowledge that must be gained before starting such a diet.

Early August (16½ Months)

I have heard so much about the nutritional value of tofu that I bought a pack today. I cubed it and sautéed it with onions and mushrooms, and served some to Mirabai with steamed broccoli and carrots. She seemed to enjoy it far more than Bob or I did. The texture was unappealing to us and the flavor was bland, but as it is healthful and inexpensive, I will experiment and incorporate it occasionally into our meals, especially since Mirabai likes it. This will also be an incentive for us to break down a few food prejudices and expand our dietary horizons.

Tofu is made from soybeans. It is rich in usable protein, contains all eight essential amino acids, and delivers over 35 percent of its calories in the form of protein. Tofu is low in saturated fats and carbohydrates, and has no cholesterol, preservatives, coloring, or additives. The little fat there is contains large amounts of lecithin and an important nutrient, linoleic acid. Besides being a good source of calcium and other minerals, such as iron, phosphorus and potassium, tofu also has essential B vitamins, choline, and the fat-soluble vitamin E. Tofu is soft, very easily digested, and an excellent food for babies.

Like yogurt or cottage cheese, tofu is ready to eat and requires no preparation. However, it is extremely versatile in cooking, and can be steamed, broiled, sautéed, toasted, or baked. Tofu can also be sliced, cubed, mashed, puréed, frozen, dried, or blended. Since it is almost tasteless, it mixes well with virtually any other ingredient and will pick up the flavor and aroma of whatever it is combined with.

Mid-August (17 Months)

It has been so hot that Mirabai has had very little appetite and is surviving primarily on milk, juices, and fruit. The mornings are still fairly cool and she has a substantial breakfast, but at lunch and dinner she eats only a little before handing me her plate saying firmly, "Away." I realize she has picked up the habit of removing her bowl, cup, or anything else on her tray, as this is something I do immediately when she has had enough. But it is a habit that I encouraged totally unconsciously.

Last week I gave Mirabai beets for lunch. Although she was very hungry, the taste and texture did not appeal to her and she wouldn't eat them. Looking around, she saw a banana in the fruit basket and indicated that she wanted it. I put some slices in her bowl and watched her alternate quite independently between the beets and banana until they had disappeared.

Developing independence, which starts about nine months of age, can be either exciting or distressing to parents. Behavior patterns may already have been formed, and from that time on, the infant will start to display them.

During the first year an infant has tremendous adjustments to make, including adapting to new foods and methods of eating. Rebellion against unfamiliar foods can be lessened and long-term refusals prevented if parents learn to recognize their children's eating patterns. For instance, the realization that an eighteen-month-old may have a sporadic appetite, and that this is no cause for undue alarm, may prevent long-lasting battles over food.

Very hot weather may cause smaller appetites. At these times, meals should be kept light. Use tuna, cheese, eggs, and other dishes that are light and easy to prepare and work well in salads. A variety of fresh fruits and vegetables can provide sufficient vitamins and minerals, especially when they are supplemented with fruit juices and milk. Fresh fruit-juice popsicles can be made in your freezer for a healthy and refreshing treat, as well as shakes made with berries, yogurt, juices, eggs, milk and/or ice cream.

Mid-September (18 Months)

Mirabai's vocabulary is expanding, walking has brought new-found freedom, and her feelings of self-confidence and independence are developing rapidly. I usually let her decide what she will eat for breakfast, and her choices so far have been reasonable. This morning she asked for cottage cheese, prunes, and banana with milk, and at lunchtime I gave her an egg, whole wheat bread, fresh steamed vegetables, and fresh fruit. She is eating less than she used to and is completely independent with feeding, countering any offers of assistance with "Bibai do it." She accepts a wide variety of foods, is healthy, and generally seems to be a contented child.

I feel she is now mentally and physically mature enough to understand some simple table manners. We add the word "Please" after each request she makes and "Thank you" when she receives what she has asked for. To my delight, everyone has become very polite at mealtimes, with pleases and thank-yous everywhere. Bob and the boys have always teased me about my insistence on good manners and what they consider to be my "bourgeois pretentiousness." That is, until now. Suddenly it has become very important that Mirabai be polite and learn "correct" table manners. So we have also added "Don't play with your food" and "Don't talk with your mouth full." These are enough rules for now, except that we always wash our hands before eating.

As Mirabai matures, we will add to her list of basic table manners: No elbows on the table, no licking fingers or knives, learning how to use utensils, using a napkin instead of her hand to wipe her mouth.

This is a perfect opportunity for all of us to take a refresher course on our own table manners and to remember that children learn best by good example.

After the rapid development of the first year, the rate of growth slows down. Important muscle development takes place as the child learns to walk. His major back, thigh, and buttock muscles must be strengthened for walking and erect posture. Bones begin to lengthen, and more of the body's mineral deposits are used to strengthen bones to carry the extra weight.

The child has an increasing sense of self, or ego, of being a distinct individual, and starts to realize that he is not just an extension of his mother. He wants to decide and act for himself, whether he is

capable of doing so or not. It is important for the parent to under-
stand two principles at this time: (1) The child is striving for auton-
omy and his attempts often take the form of refusing food and wanting
to be independent before he is able to be. Support and encouragement
should be given in self-feeding and selection of foods. The parent
should maintain a calm relaxed attitude and express a sympathetic
interest in the toddler's efforts. Give help when needed, but avoid
overprotection or excessive rigidity. (2) The child needs fewer calories
but more protein and minerals for growth. A variety of healthy foods
should be offered in smaller quantities to provide these nutrients.

By the time a child is eighteen months old, ritual becomes very
important. Acts performed the same way several times will be repeated
diligently by your child, and this can offer a marvelous opportunity
to establish positive habits. Young children copy everything adults
do, for better or worse. Although this is a very effective way to teach
children, parents may be surprised at some of the mirror images they
receive of themselves. We can learn from children, as they can learn
from us. These challenging times can be a positive experience for
everyone.

Late September (18½ Months)

Although it was a long, hot summer, we never seemed to find
time to go to the beach. With Mirabai napping at noon, there was
not enough time in the mornings, and it was too late to pack up and
go after her nap. But somehow I couldn't let a whole summer pass
without at least one trip to the beach, so, nap or no nap, we did it
today. The children are back at school, so the beaches were not
crowded, and the day was clear and sunny.

I packed a simple lunch for us both with two hard-boiled eggs,
one quartered tomato, whole wheat crackers, Jarlsberg cheese cubes,
apple juice, and a bowl of cut-up canteloupe and watermelon. Several changes of clothes (including a long-sleeved top and a sun hat),
blanket, towel, sun-block cream, and shovel and pail were crammed
into a huge straw bag, and with Mirabai, ice chest, and accessories,
we set off. Mirabai fell asleep almost immediately and although it

was a short nap, it seemed to be sufficient. As soon as we were settled on the sand, I gave her a liberal coating of sun-block cream and she set off to catch seagulls. Although her enthusiasm never flagged, it took her too far from our spot on the beach, and I had to watch her constantly and bring her back to "home base." All this running made her thirsty and gave her a wonderful appetite, so she really enjoyed her somewhat sandy egg, melon, and crackers. Although it was not exactly a restful day for Mamma, it was lovely to see her enjoying the freedom, and her happiness exhilarated me, too. A couple of hours or so was just enough time for this delightful new experience, and a tired little girl finished her nap on the way home.

An outing or a trip can be a mixed pleasure for parents. Once a child starts walking, he is going to get into everything possible, and even some things that seem impossible. The days of long adult conversations, reading, a serious game of chess or volleyball at the beach are over for a while. The focus has to shift to your little one, to sharing his activities, explorations, and pleasures. All children love the beach, parks, or mountains, and picnicking can be the highlight of the day. It is as easy to prepare a nutritious picnic with yogurt, fruit, juices, hard cheese, hard-boiled eggs, and crackers as it is to pack potato chips, sodas, cakes, and processed cheese. Raw vegetables with pita bread, breadsticks and homemade dip, pineapple spears, dried apricots and peaches, and so on, will satisfy the cravings of the fussiest appetite and the sweetest tooth, with the added bonus of providing more fiber, vitamins, minerals, and lower calories than almost any processed food.

Small jars or bottles can be filled with fresh lemonade, orange, grape, or apple juice and put in the freezer the night before an outing. By the time you arrive at your destination you will have either fruit slushes or icy cold drinks, depending on how far you are traveling and how hot the weather is. A little more thought may be necessary to prepare fresh foods than to open a bag of cookies or potato chips, but the benefits to your child's health—to say nothing of the good eating habits that are encouraged—make it well worthwhile.

Mid-October (19 Months)

I had enjoyed Marion Cunningham's cooking class so much that I decided to try another on bread making. Although I have made bread several times, I have never been very satisfied with the results, so I hoped to find out some trade secrets. Today I decided to put my newfound knowledge to the test and I baked her Health Bread (see page 252). It turned out beautifully—light, tasty, and with a good crust—and I felt very pleased with myself.

Mirabai loves bread and butter but always leaves the crust. She certainly has enough teeth to handle crust, so I refuse to trim it off in hopes that one day she will discover that that is the best part of a loaf. She and I are the only ones in the family who prefer whole-grain breads, as Bob's favorites are French and Italian breads, and William swears by the ultrawhite, sponge-soft kind. However, when I serve home-baked bread, everyone loves it.

Bread is a staple food in many cultures around the world. It is made in a vast variety of shapes and sizes with equally various grains and flours: East Indian chapatis, Middle Eastern pita bread, Mexican tortillas, and Norwegian lefse, to mention a few—all of these are flat unleavened breads made from wheat, corn, or potatoes. Through the ages, different breads were made for various classes of people, with white bread being reserved solely for the nobility.

White bread achieves its fine texture through the bran and germ being removed from the wheat, which reduces its value as a food source. Since 1970, sales of white "enriched" bread have been dropping, and there is a growing awareness that whole-grain breads offer more nutritional value than fortified white bread. The kernel of the wheat plant has an outer layer, the bran, which contains the germ and endosperm. Bran is composed of starch, protein, oil, cellulose, fiber, minerals such as calcium and iron, and vitamins E and the B complex. When the bran and wheat germ are removed from white flour, many nutrients are removed with them. To make this flour even whiter and longer lasting, it is then bleached. Some millers replace the lost vitamins and mineals with synthetic nutrients, although the bran is not restored. Bran is valuable for its fiber, an element that is undesirably low in the American diet. Lack of fiber in nutrition has been linked to diseases like diverticulitis, obesity, gallstones, heart disease, colorectal cancer, polyps, and hiatus hernia.

With more public awareness of good nutrition, millers and bakers are adapting to the demand for a variety of whole wheat breads and unbleached white flour, as well as stone-ground whole wheat flour. Other flours for use in bread making (some alone, some combined with wheat) are graham, rye, oat, barley, buckwheat, corn, soy, rice, bran, millet, gluten, and potato. It is no longer difficult to buy good, healthful bread in America. Should you have time to make your own, however, you will not only get all the nutrients you want but also discover how delicious bread can really be.

Late October—Halloween (19½ Months)

It is Halloween, the most dreaded day of the year for me, not because of the "tricks" but because of the "treats." When my sons were children, they would return from trick or treating with pillowcases full of candy. Although I was able to appeal to their noble side and persuade them to give most of it to Children's Hospital, it is a custom I prefer not to start with Mirabai. So I have been dreaming up different ways of celebrating Halloween without the emphasis on candy. I bought little packages of roasted peanuts and raisins for children who come to the house, as well as three pumpkins which Robert and William have carved into lanterns. I also roasted the pumpkin seeds as treats for ourselves. Mirabai is fascinated by the children in their costumes and enjoys helping me hand out the nuts and raisins.

I realize that Halloween is a very exciting time for children, so I will try to come up with something special next year, possibly a Halloween-at-Home party with some little friends. We can make puppets, witches, ghosts and goblins, to tell the tale of Halloween, and visit a few close neighbors for trick or treat. Unfortunately, today there are many psychotic people in our society who tamper with the candy or fruit they hand out, and it is essential that parents check their children's treats carefully. Unless given by friends or neighbors who are personally known to the family, any treat that is not factory sealed should be discarded.

Next year I will make Mirabai a costume, and as she grows older, we may get into the tradition of fortune telling. I am sure she will have her own ideas, too. One day I may even look forward to Halloween instead of dreading it.

Halloween, or All Hallows Eve, bears little resemblance today to its point of origin, the Celtic new year's eve, a Druid ritual of fire and remembrance of the dead through the worship of the pagan god Samhain. Bonfires were lit to help the dying sun whose rays grew feeble at this time of year, when the human psyche was at its lowest. Through dance, meditation, and chanting, witches believed they were able to renew their physical energy and psychic forces. These rituals were later adapted to Christian ceremonies, becoming feasts in honor of all saints, All Hallows. Elves, fairies, and witches (who sometimes took the shape of cats) were believed to fly on All Hallows Eve, and large bonfires were set to ward off these spirits. Halloween was also thought to be the most favorable time for fortune telling and apples and nuts were used for this purpose.

Irish and Scottish immigrants brought Halloween traditions with them to the United States during the late nineteenth century. In this country, a pumpkin replaced the turnip or potato used for carving jack-o'-lanterns. Bobbing for apples in a pail of water replaced their use in fortune telling. The Irish believed that "the little people" play pranks during Halloween; this started the custom of boys and men playing practical jokes on that night.

With children today wearing costumes and going from door to door to trick or treat, some safety measures should be kept in mind. Encourage the use of light-colored costumes, or sew on reflecting tape front and back, so the children can be easily seen by motorists. If costumes are homemade, purchase only flame-retardant material. As masks may block a child's vision, use makeup to paint a mask on his face or at least enlarge the eye apertures in the mask to ensure maximum vision. Young trick-or-treaters should always be accompanied by an adult and carry a flashlight after dusk.

Mid-November (20 Months)

The Norwegian Seamen's Church is having its annual Christmas Bazaar this week. It is so far away from where we live, I visit only once a year, usually at the holiday season. Close to the church is a Norwegian import store, so I also stock up on all the traditional foods that are a part of our Christmas celebrations. This year we decided to pick up Bob from work and drive down to the church in the late afternoon. Mirabai took a long nap, and as she did not have time to eat before we left, I made up some little individual food bags for the long journey. One bag contained a peeled and quartered pear, another several stoned-wheat crackers, a third had two quarters of a tomato, and the last contained three small cubes of Swiss cheese. A child's vacuum flask, the kind that has a little spout, was filled with milk so that Mirabai could drink by herself without spilling.

Having lost my way to Bob's office, I was then relieved of the driving by an anxious father. By this time Mirabai was hungry, so I gave her the little bags, one at a time, which she thought was fun and enjoyed opening. After finishing everything, she sat happily and quietly for the rest of the journey.

When we arrived at the church, we found a wonderful *smørgåsbord* of the most delicious open-faced sandwiches imaginable. They included hard-boiled eggs with anchovies, lox and scrambled eggs, *karbonade* (a kind of meat cake) with fried onions, pâté with beets and cucumber, and lots more. Mirabai was full and not at all interested, so I ate for both of us, but she did taste my *bløtkake* (sponge cake with fresh fruit and whipped cream), which is irresistible even if the tummy is full.

Traveling with children can be enjoyable and memorable. Without careful planning and consideration, however, it can also be a disaster. What is needed for a journey depends on the length of the trip, the age of your children, and the type of transportation. Some general rules apply, regardless of certain specifics.

For each child it is easiest to have a large bag containing the following:

- *A complete change of clothing, extra diapers, wet towelettes, facial tissues, and a warm sweater or coat*
- *Individual bags containing simple foods that will not spoil, are easy to consume, and are usually enjoyed by the child. Raw or cooked vegetables and fruits, hard cheeses, crackers, or toast are good basics. Juice, milk, and water should be taken in a vacuum flask. Prefrozen cans of juice are handy if the weather is very warm. Bottles with disposable liners are good for infants on trips, as there is no need to sterilize bottles.*
- *A variety of toys in simple containers such as plastic bowls with lids or a cloth drawstring bag, keeping in mind your child's age and limitations of space and movement while traveling*
- *When flying with infants, keep several bottles of juice or milk handy for ascending and descending. (Swallowing minimizes the possibility of earaches or other discomforts.)*

The success of a trip depends most of all on your own attitude and state of mind. If you can relax, be flexible, understand an infant's restlessness and tiredness, give him a lot of attention (singing songs, telling stories, and encouraging him to observe the changing scenery when possible), the trip can be enjoyable for everyone.

Early December (20½ Months)

We are having spaghetti for dinner tonight, a family favorite. Mirabai is very hungry and walking underfoot while I am preparing it, saying over and over again, "Bibai have 'getti." It is driving me slightly mad. I suppose repetition is part of this stage of development, but I hope she grows out of it soon. My sons untactfully remind me that I do the same thing, but the comparison is unfair. At least I let hours and even days pass between my reiterations.

I knew that neither Mirabai nor I would be able to wait for dinner, so I boiled a handful of spinach pastina. This dish took only five minutes to cook and looked lovely served with tomato sauce. Mirabai hesitated to eat it because it wasn't the spaghetti she had expected, but hunger ruled and she finished it as well as a small lettuce and tomato salad.

Pasta belongs to one of the four basic food groups we need each day, the bread-cereal group that provides starch, bulk and proteins, vitamins and minerals. Pasta supplies us with carbohydrates. Made predominantly from wheat, it may contain other ingredients, such as soy, eggs, and spinach. Pasta plays an important role in the Italian diet, and there are many dozens of different shapes and types. All supermarkets carry a variety of macaroni products, but for the best selection it is worthwhile finding an Italian market.

Most children love pasta and there are limitless ways to serve it, from a simple spaghetti with olive oil and garlic to salad primavera. For infants and toddlers there is a special pastina (tiny dough) that can be prepared as a breakfast cereal with milk and raisins or fruit. It can also be mixed with formula, milk, or butter, served as a side dish, added to soups, or mixed with vegetables. There are several other small pastas that children love, including stelline (little stars), alphabet, acini di pepe (peppercorns), orzo (rice-shaped), semi di mellone (apple or melon seeds), tubettini (small hollow tubes), ditalini (larger hollow tubes), and rotelle (small wheels). They all mix well with squash, lentils, beans, fresh peas, chick peas, broccoli, or spinach as well as with traditional tomato or meat sauces and fish, cheese, and meat dishes.

If your child rejects a specific vegetable, he may accept it if mixed with pasta. With some experimentation, you will find unlimited combinations of this versatile food from which your child will choose his own favorites.

Mid-December (21 Months)

Christmas is rapidly approaching and today Mirabai tried her hand at making Christmas cookies for the first time with some help from Mommy, William, and her little friend Daniel. I prepared the mixture for *sirup snipper* (ginger snaps), a traditional Norwegian Christmas cookie, and let the children make the designs either freehand or with cookie cutters. William made a spectacular space shuttle, Daniel produced a tray of Santas, angels, stars, and trees, plus "E.T.," and Mirabai had a wonderful time pounding a piece of dough into a grayish rubbery substance until William taught her how to cut out a Santa Claus. After our creations had been in the oven for a few minutes, the house was filled with the wonderful aromas that remind me of past holidays.

Mirabai barely touched her dinner, having eaten too many cookies, not to mention a lot of raw dough. But for once I didn't worry, as she was having such a good time. Later we lit the fire and made popcorn, some of which we ate. The rest we threaded along with cranberries to trim the tree. Robert and his girl friend made little paper baskets to hang on the tree that were filled with nuts, raisins, licorice, and chocolate. We placed them up high and told Mirabai that the chocolate was for Santa. Bob got into the spirit of things with a rousing and somewhat inaccurate version of *Jingle Bells*, so I started to play some Christmas songs on the piano. Mirabai crawled up beside me on the piano stool, and with her help Bob and I sang a duet: the first time in our twenty-year marriage that we have ever done such a thing.

Mirabai was too tired to help with the finishing touches on the Christmas tree, and after one more song was quite willing to be put to bed. As I tucked her in, she gave me a beautiful smile and said, "I like cookies, Mamma."

Most Americans prize their cultural backgrounds, especially the traditions and foods associated with them. As certain ethnic foods may be difficult to obtain and their preparation very time-consuming, many such dishes are prepared only on special holidays. At these times I feel nutrition can take a backseat. Throughout the human life cycle, food and eating serve not only to meet nutritional requirements, but are also important for personal psychosocial development. Conversation, warmth, and a happy atmosphere are as important as the food served.

Early January (22½ Months)

For Mirabai's lunch today I wanted to try something different, so I thought we would have fish. Growing up in Norway, where wonderful fish was served almost daily, has made me so particular about

quality and freshness that I seldom buy it here. However, it is not
fair to deprive my family of this versatile and nutritious food they
all love. So today I prepared some fillets of sole and fresh spinach
for our lunch. I steamed the sole, washed the spinach and boiled it
for five minutes in the water clinging to the leaves, and cooked a
few carrots. Everything was ready in a few minutes, and I served it
unseasoned with a dot of unsalted butter. Mirabai finished it all
with apparent pleasure, and then had a baked apple with raisins
and milk for dessert.

*As our society becomes more calorie and nutrition conscious, fish
is becoming a frequent part of the diet. Fish is low in calories, and
it is an excellent source of easily digested, high-quality protein, containing more polyunsaturated than saturated fats. The vitamin content varies with the species, but fish generally is a good source of
riboflavin, niacin, and vitamin B_{12}. The fattier types of fish also supply the fat-soluble vitamin D. Fish contains significant amounts of
phosphorus, potassium, magnesium, and iron, and is low in sodium.
(Even saltwater fish are not high in sodium.) Because fish contains
little connective tissue it is easy to digest and suitable for most diets.*

*Although fish is an excellent food source, many cooks resist pre-
paring it, perhaps because they lack knowledge on how to cook it.
Fish, when properly cooked, becomes opaque and flakes easily with a
fork. Overcooking makes the flesh dry and tough. A good rule of
thumb for judging if fish is perfectly cooked has been developed by
the Canadian Department of Fisheries: Measure the fish at its thick-
est point. Allow ten minutes' cooking time for each inch of thickness
for fresh fish, twenty minutes per inch for frozen fish. Fish may be
cooked without thawing, except for layered fillets, which need to be
partially thawed so that they can be separated. If fish is cooked in
oil or a sauce, allow an extra five minutes per inch. Since there are
many variables, always test fish to ensure that it is cooked through.*

*Another deterrent for many people is dealing with the skin and
bones. Small bones are especially dangerous for young children. In
Norway there was a method of preparing fish that was very popular
when I was a child. It contained no skin or bones. Fish fillets were*

ground and made into a thick purée from which fish pudding, fish balls, or fish cakes could be made. I remember that my parents would need to set aside a whole day to prepare such dishes. Today, using a food processor, and with fish already skinned and boned, preparation would take little more than half an hour. For adults this may not be the most appealing way to eat fish, as it is somewhat bland, but toddlers and children love it.

I was looking through an old Norwegian cookbook recently and found some of the following recipes listed in the index: Fish cotelettes, Fish pâté, Fish filets Béarnaise, Fish fricassee, Fish au gratin, Fish fried à la Mignon, Fish ragu, Fish roulettes, Fish Wienerschnitzel. You can see that in Scandinavia fish is prepared in many ways we usually think of as reserved for meat. This does show that there is a large variety of ways in which fish can be served. If you are willing to experiment and are open to new flavors and textures, nutrition and mealtimes can both gain new dimensions.

Mid-February (23 Months)

It has been raining almost daily for months now, quite a phenomenon for Southern California, and we have been using the fireplace frequently. The sounds of wood crackling and rain against the windows and the coziness of the living room are all invitations for hot chocolate, popcorn, and a good book in front of the fire. This evening I made Bob cocoa with artificial sweetener, hot chocolate for the boys, and Mirabai and I had carob milk. Everyone had his own bowl of popcorn.

Mirabai loves these special evenings. Tonight we all took turns reading a story from her little library, which is geared toward two-year-olds. When the boys were very young we did the same thing, and I remember that fairy tales from other lands became great favorites. As they grew older the books matured with them. I later realized that reading aloud to the boys from a very early age helped lay the foundations for their love of reading. If I was not able to finish a story for two or three days, they became impatient to know the ending. Once they had learned to read, they would painstak-

ingly work their way through the pages and soon were very profi-
cient readers. But on rainy days we would still read aloud in front
of the fire while sipping hot chocolate and eating popcorn.

*Carob is a good substitute for chocolate. If you start your child on
it, he will enjoy the flavor and eventually choose it over cocoa or
chocolate. Carob powder is made from the dried pods of the carob
tree, and its texture is similar to that of cocoa, although different in
taste and nutritional value. It is higher in natural sugars, crude fiber
and iron, and lower in calories, crude fat, and sodium. Carob can
be used as a substitute for cocoa or chocolate, and in recipes calling
for cocoa the cocoa can be replaced by an equivalent amount of
carob. When substituting chocolate in cooking, use 3 tablespoonsful
of carob powder plus 1 tablespoonful of water for each square of
chocolate. Carob blends well with other flavors and is especially good
with orange, lemon, vanilla, and almond.*

*Not everyone has a fireplace, but family evenings with a warm
atmosphere can be created in any household. Such occasions will
linger in the memory for a lifetime. If pastimes, like games, reading,
singing, crafts, or discussions, are part of the evening, a love for such
activities will be fostered in your child in later years. This is worth
keeping in mind especially when encouraging enthusiastic and pro-
ficient readers.*

Mid-March (2 Years Old)

It is Mirabai's birthday and we are having a big party. I am not
only celebrating her birthday but also the birth of this book, since
we just signed the contract with our publisher. (Without Mirabai,
however, there would have been no book!) We are inviting all the
friends who have given encouragement, inspiration, or positive critiques. I have prepared a vegetarian lasagna, a huge green salad,
and a Norwegian birthday cake. Jeannie is fixing some kind of ex-
otic Thai chicken dish and a *tabbouleh* salad, Jana has made fruit
salad, and Benita is bringing handmade chocolate baskets filled
with chocolate-dipped strawberries and white-chocolate baskets full

of delicious truffles and chocolates. To round out the buffet, we have lots of French bread and butter, wine, and soft drinks for the children.

I keep thinking that this is not a children's party, although there will be six of them present. It is basically my celebration of Mirabai's birth and the two years of love and happiness she has given us.

The Limoges china and crystal used for special occasions are dusted off and the silver has been shined. We have camellias, Easter lilies, and iris from the garden in every room in the house, and a fire is going in the living room because it is pouring rain outside. Two wonderful friends, Fay and Barbara, arrived early this morning and with a speed, efficiency, and harmony rarely seen, cleaned, washed, polished, set the table, and decorated the house, leaving me time to prepare the food.

Mirabai knows something very special is happening today, her second birthday, and I am worried that she will be too excited to nap. But it is as if she knows she needs to sleep in order to be up this evening and goes willingly to bed, taking a three-hour nap. By the time she wakes up, Daddy is home. He gives her a bath, washes her hair, and dresses her in the prettiest dress she owns.

By the time the first guests arrive everything is ready, including me. This is a first! For once I don't have to greet my guests shoeless or with my hair uncombed. Mirabai opens her presents as each person arrives. In this way, it will not be too overwhelming for her and she can appreciate each gift and the person it is from. She is delighted when the children arrive, especially little Robert, who is three and a favorite friend. They wander off into Mirabai's room to play with her toys. All the children are well behaved but still having a good time. William and Daniel have disappeared. They are turning a cardboard box and bits of electrical gadgetry into a car and appear only to have their plates and glasses refilled. Little Christopher, also two, appears *au naturel,* informing his mother that his diapers were wet so he took them off. The adults, who range from eighteen to eighty-plus, are tucking into the food, socializing, and enjoying themselves.

Although Jeannie has done her utmost to talk me out of giving my little speech, I insist; so everyone's glass gets filled and the room becomes quiet. I give thanks and propose toasts for all the inspiration, ideas, and help given to *The Baby Cookbook*, and Mirabai gets her "Happy Birthday" song with much clapping, kissing, and hugs, and she is loving every minute of it. She is also very tired. Although the party is not over, she doesn't resist being put to bed. Soon other parents with children leave, and by the time the embers from the fire die down, the last guest says good-bye. It is the end of a busy, wonderful day. It is also the end of Mirabai's first two years in this world. We are entering into a new era, The Terrible Twos! But the memories of the last two years give me nothing but joy.

FAMILY RECIPES AND SPECIAL CHILDREN'S RECIPES

Notes on the Recipes

MOST of the recipes that follow you would expect to find in an adult cookbook, not in *The Baby Cookbook*. So why are they included here? There are two reasons.

First, by the time your baby is twelve months old, he can share family meals. It is then important that he be exposed to as wide a variety of healthy foods as possible. Through a varied diet, he will acquire the taste for many foods from each of the four food groups, which should give him total nutrition. Your child's pleasure in eating will also be expanded and you will be discouraging him from becoming a finicky eater

Second, *The Baby Cookbook* family recipes have been designed to be low in sodium (salt); they contain almost no sugar or refined sweeteners, emphasize high-quality foods and healthy methods of preparation, and are generally geared toward encouraging good eating habits. (Some adults may wish to add more salt and seasonings to suit their own tastes. This should be done only *after* your child's portion has been set aside for him. Your baby does not have your taste buds and does not need added salt.)

Recipes designed especially for very young children are mingled with family recipes that they can share when they are a little older, because, after all, your baby is certainly a member of the family! and all the family cooking takes place in one kitchen.

However, so that you can locate the special recipes for babies, the "serving" line at the bottom of those recipes is printed in **bold-face type** (such as **1 child serving**), and the titles of the recipes are identified in the same way in the Recipe Index. If you are alone with your baby at lunch or supper, there are some recipes that *you* can share with him: The serving line reads **1 adult and 1 child serving.** Or you can use such a recipe to make child portions for several meals.

Servings in the adult recipes vary in number so that the recipes can be used for two, four, six, or more people, or can be divided into two or more meals—one for now, the remainder for tomorrow's lunch or the freezer (which will help working mothers). A few recipes are for parties, to serve lots of people, and your child may have his share of those, too. All servings shown for adults are large enough to include some for your child, as he will need no more than one or two tablespoonsful of each food from the meal.

You will discover that cooking well for the whole family is a great timesaver as your baby becomes a toddler and shares in family meals instead of having his food cooked for him separately.

PREPARATION OF BASIC FOODS

Dried Beans

There are two methods of preparing dried beans: One is to cook them without soaking; the other is to soak them overnight, which will considerably shorten the cooking time. In fact, unsoaked beans take twice as long to cook and twice as much water to prepare; there is also a greater risk of their burning or cooking dry, as they absorb the water more rapidly than presoaked beans.

A faster method than soaking beans overnight is to boil them in water for 2 minutes and then allow to stand for 1 hour.

There is some dispute whether the water used for soaking should be saved or not, as it may contain valuable nutrients. According to the California Dry Bean Advisory Board, the nutrient loss is minimal when you discard the water. In addition to getting rid of impurities such as dirt or stones, soaking reduces flatus-causing factors, which are washed out in the soaking water (thus improving the digestibility of beans). The protein value of the beans is not affected, so it would seem advisable to discard the water.

Adding 1 tablespoonful of oil for each cup of beans during presoaking will reduce foaming that occurs when the beans are boiling.

One cup of dried beans will make about 3 cups of cooked beans.

2¼ cups dry beans (1 lb.), presoaked	OR, FOR SMALLER QUANTITY: *1 cup dry beans, presoaked*
7 cups water	*4 cups water*
2 tsp. salt (optional)	*½ tsp. salt (optional)*

METHOD ONE:

Bring water to a boil in a heavy kettle, with salt if desired. Beans should first be sorted carefully and washed in cold water and drained. Add beans to boiling water, return to a boil, and cook over high heat for 2 minutes. Remove from heat and let stand for at least 1 hour. Drain, rinse, replace water, and bring to a boil again. Reduce heat and simmer, covered, until tender (from 1 to 2 hours depending on the type of bean). Drain.

METHOD TWO:

Add presoaked beans to rapidly boiling water. Return to boil, reduce heat, cover, and simmer until tender. Drain.

In both methods check during cooking to ensure that beans do not burn or dry out. If too much water evaporates, add more as necessary.

/ / /

Lentils

Lentils do not require soaking before cooking. Using 1 cup of lentils to 3 cups of water, these legumes can be prepared in the same way as dried beans (Method Two). Cooking time will be between 40 to 60 minutes.

One cup of uncooked lentils will make about 2 cups of cooked lentils.

/ / /

Tomatoes
(How to Blanch and Peel)

Add a whole tomato to a small pan of boiling water. Remove from heat. Let stand for 1 minute. Remove with a slotted spoon, cool a little, then remove skin with a sharp paring knife.

/ / /

Stewed Fruit

Clean, pit, and peel fruit. Use ripe sweet fruits such as apples, peaches, plums, etc. Place fruit with enough water to cover in a small saucepan. Gently bring to a boil, reduce heat and simmer until tender, around 10 to 15 minutes. Drain off liquid, or use when puréeing the fruit.

If the fruit is too sharp or acid for your baby, add a little mashed banana or papaya.

Dried fruits may be stewed. It is not necessary, or easy, to peel them. Use the same method as for fresh fruits, although cooking times may vary a little.

/ / /

Homemade Yogurt

2 cups whole milk
¼ cup dry nonfat milk
*Bulgarian yogurt starter (obtainable in freeze-dried packet from health-
food stores)*

Check directions on yogurt starter packet for how much to use for
2 cups milk. Mix whole and nonfat milks together in a saucepan
and heat almost to boiling point. Remove from heat and cool to
90°–100° (test with food thermometer). Add yogurt starter and stir
until completely dissolved. Pour mixture into a meticulously clean
container, cover with lid, and keep warm until yogurt is set. (I keep
mine warm on the top of the stove with a sweater wrapped around
it.) After 6 to 8 hours, when yogurt is firm, place in refrigerator
and let stand overnight.

For the next batch of yogurt, use a tablespoonful from this recipe as a starter.

Makes about 2 cups

/ / /

Paneer
(Homemade Cottage Cheese)

½ gallon whole or low-fat milk
Juice of 2 lemons

Bring milk to a foaming boil over medium heat and add the lemon
juice. Stir together briefly and allow milk to boil for a few more
seconds until it curdles. Remove pan from heat and let stand until
curds and whey separate (2 to 3 minutes). Using a clean cheese-

cloth or sieve, strain off liquid and refrigerate cheese in a covered container until needed.

Be sure to save whey liquid to use in soups or drinks. It is highly nutritious.

Makes ½ cup

VEGETABLES

Baked Acorn Squash

1 acorn (or butternut) squash
2 tbsp. butter

Scrub squash, halve, and scoop out seeds. Put 1 tablespoon butter in each half and place in an ovenproof dish containing 1 inch of water. Cover with foil and bake in preheated 350° oven for about 1 hour, or until tender. Remove flesh from shells and mash, adding more butter, or milk, if needed.

Salt and pepper may be added for adults, if desired.

Serves 2

/ / /

Asparagus with Parmesan Cheese

1 bunch fresh asparagus, washed and trimmed
⅓ cup freshly grated Parmesan cheese
2 tbsp. olive oil

Stand asparagus upright in a tall saucepan half filled with boiling water, and cook until semisoft but the bottoms of the spears are still firm when tested with a knife. Drain well and arrange in a baking dish. Baste with the olive oil and sprinkle with the Parmesan cheese. Bake in preheated 400° oven for about 10 minutes, or until cheese browns.

Serves 4

/ / /

Avocado and Papaya Salad

1 ripe avocado   *½ ripe papaya*

DRESSING:

¼ cup lime juice   *⅛ tsp. pepper*
1 tsp. salt   *½ cup olive oil*

Peel and seed avocado and papaya and slice into a bowl. Mix together lime juice, salt, and pepper, and stir in olive oil until blended. Use half of dressing to cover salad (reserving remainder in refrigerator for another use).

Dressing may be omitted for young children, if preferred.

Serves 2

/ / /

Stuffed Bell Peppers

4 large bell peppers, washed,
   tops removed, and seeded
3 tbsp. butter
1 small onion, peeled and
   chopped
12 mushrooms, washed and
   sliced
1 cup cooked rice

¼ cup seedless raisins
½ cup bread crumbs
1½ cups canned tomatoes,
   crushed
4 tbsp. grated cheddar cheese
1 cup tomato sauce (optional;
   see page 283)

Set peppers in a pan of boiling water for 1 minute. Remove and
place in ovenproof baking dish. Melt butter in a skillet and sauté
onion and mushrooms until tender. Add rice, raisins, bread crumbs,
sautéed onion, and tomatoes and mix well, but do not cook. With
a spoon narrow enough to fit inside the peppers, fill each pepper to
the top with mixture. Add ¼ cup water to baking dish and cook
peppers in preheated 350° oven for 30 minutes. Eight minutes before peppers are done, sprinkle tops with grated cheese. Serve with
tomato sauce, if desired.

Serves 4

/ / /

Broccoli Indian Style

½ lb. broccoli, washed and cut
   up
1 tbsp. safflower or peanut oil
1 tsp. mustard seeds
1 onion, peeled and chopped
1 tsp. turmeric

½ tsp. coriander
1 tsp. garam masala (from Far
   Eastern grocery store; or see
   page 153)
1 tbsp. lemon juice
2 tbsp. plain yogurt

1 tbsp. shredded coconut   2 tomatoes, peeled and chopped
¼ cup water   (optional)

Steam broccoli for 5 minutes (it should still be quite firm). In pan
heat oil and add mustard seeds. Stir while they pop, then reduce
heat to medium, add onion, and sauté until tender. Add turmeric,
coriander, *garam masala*, lemon juice, yogurt, coconut, and water
(also tomatoes, if desired). Mix well, bring to a boil, and add broccoli. Reduce heat and let simmer for 5 minutes, or until flavors
have blended and broccoli is tender.

Serves 2

/ / /

Garam Masala
(Indian Seasoning)

Seeds from 2 cardamom pods   2 tsp. whole cumin seed
30 whole peppercorns   (optional)
1 tsp. whole cloves   2-inch piece cinnamon stick

Grind all ingredients as finely as possible, using either a mortar
and pestle or a nut grinder. Store in an airtight container, as this
supply will last some time.

/ / /

Brussels Sprouts and Carrots in Lemon Butter

½ lb. Brussels sprouts, trimmed
and halved
½ lb. carrots, scrubbed, and
halved lengthwise and
crosswise

4 tbsp. butter
1 small clove garlic, minced
Juice and grated peel of ¼
lemon

Steam Brussels sprouts and carrots for 10 minutes. Drain and arrange in a heated serving dish. Melt butter with garlic, add lemon juice and peel, and pour over vegetables. (Save stock from vegetables for other recipes.)

Serves 4

/ / /

Carrot Apple Purée

1 carrot, scrubbed and sliced
1 apple, peeled, cored, and sliced
2 tbsp. milk
½ tsp. butter

Steam carrot and apple slices until tender. Purée or mash with milk and butter.

2 or 3 child servings

/ / /

Carrots and Beets with Apple

2 medium-size carrots, scrubbed   ½ apple, cored, washed, and diced
   and thinly sliced   ⅓ cup apple juice
2 small cooked beets, diced   1 tbsp. finely chopped parsley

Simmer carrots, beets, and apple in apple juice until tender, about
10 minutes. Purée or mash to desired consistency and top with
parsley.

1 adult and 1 child serving

/ / /

Carrot Raita

8 oz. plain yogurt (see page 149 for the homemade)
½ carrot, scrubbed and finely grated
1 tbsp. raisins, soaked in water for 30 minutes
Dash ground cardamom

Whip yogurt lightly in a bowl. Add carrot, soaked and drained raisins,
and a tiny dash of cardamom, and mix well. Chill before serving.

1 adult and 1 child serving

/ / /

Cauliflower with Avocado-Tahini Dressing

1 large head cauliflower, green leaves removed, washed and left whole
1 bay leaf
1 ripe avocado, peeled and pitted
1 cup tahini dressing (see page 284)

Place cauliflower in a steamer, add bay leaf, and steam until tender but still firm. Remove bay leaf and place cauliflower in a preheated dish. Mash avocado and mix with tahini dressing until smooth. Pour over cauliflower and serve immediately.

Serves 6

/ / /

Pineapple Coleslaw

½ cup plain yogurt
¼ cup mayonnaise
2 cups shredded cabbage

½ cup grated carrot
½ cup fresh or canned crushed pineapple, drained

Mix yogurt with mayonnaise in a large bowl. Combine cabbage, carrots, and pineapple, and stir into yogurt-mayonnaise mixture, blending well. Chill.

Serves 6

/ / /

Cucumber Salad

1 large cucumber, peeled and   1 tsp. dill
    thinly sliced   ½ tsp. salt
1 cup plain yogurt   Dash white pepper

Put cucumber in a bowl, sprinkle with salt, and let stand for 1
hour. Drain off any accumulated liquid, add yogurt, dill, and salt
and pepper, and blend well. May be chilled before serving.

Serves 3 to 4

/ / /

Eggplant Parmesan

2 medium-size eggplant,   2 cups tomato sauce (see page
    unpeeled   283)
Salt for preparation of eggplant   1 lb. mozzarella cheese, thinly
Olive oil   sliced
                                   ¼ lb. Parmesan cheese, grated

Wash eggplant and cut into slices ¾ inch thick. Lay slices on paper towels, sprinkle with salt, and cover with more towels. Weight
down with heavy pots, etc., and let stand for 1 to 2 hours. Then
brush liberally with olive oil and put under preheated broiler to
brown, turning once.

   Cover bottom of a lasagne pan, or other large ovenproof dish,
with thin layer of tomato sauce, cover this with layer of eggplant
slices, add more sauce and a layer of mozzarella, and sprinkle with
Parmesan cheese. Repeat the layers one more time, and cover dish
with foil. Bake in preheated 350° oven for 30 minutes, or until
sauce bubbles and cheese is melted. Serve immediately.

Serves 6

/ / /

Sweet and Savory Eggplant

½ cucumber, peeled and
  halved lengthwise
¼ cup olive or corn oil
1 clove garlic, finely chopped
1 medium-size eggplant,
  unpeeled, washed, and cubed

1 bell pepper, washed, seeded,
  and thinly sliced
1 tsp. tarragon
2 tomatoes, peeled and chopped
⅓ cup fresh or canned crushed
  pineapple
2 tbsp. chopped parsley

Cut cucumber into ½-inch slices. Heat oil in a large skillet, add garlic, eggplant, pepper, cucumber, and tarragon, mix well, and simmer over low flame until all ingredients are tender. Add chopped tomatoes and pineapple, mix well, and heat through. Sprinkle with parsley and serve with rice.

Serves 2

/ / /

Green Beans with Walnuts

2 tbsp. olive oil
1 clove garlic, mashed
¼ cup ground walnuts
1 cup French-style green beans, cooked

Heat oil in a frying pan, add mashed garlic, ground walnuts, and green beans. Mix gently and toss beans until well blended and heated through.

Serves 2

/ / /

Indian Vegetables with Rice

4 tbsp. safflower oil
1 tsp. mustard seeds
1 large clove garlic, crushed
1 medium-size onion, peeled
   and sliced thin
3 potatoes, peeled and chopped
5 carrots, scraped and chopped
½ head each cabbage and
   cauliflower, washed and
   chopped
1 small bunch broccoli, washed
   and cut into flowerets

1 cup tomato sauce (see page
   283) or canned tomato sauce
1 tsp. sesame salt
1-inch piece fresh ginger,
   grated, or ½ tsp. ground
   ginger
½ tsp. chili powder
2 tomatoes, peeled (if desired)
   and chopped
Parsley, chopped for garnish

Heat oil in a large heavy pan, add mustard seeds, and cook until they pop. Add garlic and onion, and cook until glazed. Add potatoes and sauté gently for 5 minutes. Add carrots, cauliflower, cabbage, and broccoli to pan, plus tomato sauce, sesame salt, ginger, and chili powder. Simmer until vegetables are tender, adding stock or water as needed. Add chopped tomatoes at the last minute. Serve over rice on a heated platter, and sprinkle with chopped parsley.

Serves 4 to 6

/ / /

Stuffed Mushrooms

6 large mushrooms, washed,
   stems removed
1 tbsp. butter

½ cup grated cheddar cheese
3 tsp. bread crumbs
1 tbsp. chopped parsley

Cover mushroom caps with boiling water for 2 minutes, drain, and dry. Place mushrooms in a buttered pie dish, put a pat of butter inside each cap, and pop under preheated broiler until almost tender. Add a generous helping of grated cheese to each cap, sprinkle with bread crumbs, and return to broiler until cheese is melted and crisp. Garnish with parsley and serve immediately.

Serves 2 to 3

/ / /

Green Peas with Pineapple

½ cup green peas, fresh or frozen
1 tbsp. finely chopped fresh or canned pineapple
1 small ripe tomato, peeled and finely chopped

In a small saucepan put peas, pineapple, and tomato, including juices from pineapple and tomato. Cook over low heat until tender, stirring occasionally. Purée or mash to desired consistency.

2 or 3 child servings

/ / /

Heavenly Potato

1 large potato, peeled
3 tbsp. cream, warmed (not boiled)
2 tbsp. grated cheddar cheese
1 tbsp. butter, melted

Boil potato until soft and mash with cream. Put into a small heat-proof dish, top with grated cheese, and cover with the melted butter. Pop under preheated broiler until cheese is melted and serve.

1 adult and 1 child serving

/ / /

Peruvian Potatoes

8 oz. cream cheese
4 hard-boiled egg yolks
¼ cup olive oil
1 cup cream (or half-and-half)

½ cup finely chopped onions
6 medium-size potatoes, cooked
   and sliced

Using a wooden spoon, cream the cheese and gradually blend in the egg yolks. Add oil a teaspoonful at a time and beat into mixture, followed by the cream and onions. Carefully fold potato slices into mixture, stir gently, then pour into a greased 1½-quart casserole. Bake in preheated 325° oven for 30 minutes.

Serves 6

/ / /

Swedish Potato Pancakes

1 medium-size potato, peeled and grated
1 egg, beaten
2 tsp. flour
1 tbsp. vegetable oil

Squeeze all moisture from grated potato. Add beaten egg and flour to potato and mix well. Heat oil in a skillet, add potato mixture by tablespoonful, and fry pancakes until brown. Turn and continue to cook until brown on the other side. Serve with applesauce or mashed banana.

Makes 6 small pancakes

/ / /

Mashed Rutabaga and Carrots

1 small rutabaga, peeled and cubed
2 carrots, scrubbed and sliced
1 tbsp. butter
Dash white pepper (optional)

Steam rutabaga and carrots until tender. Mash vegetables with butter and pepper to desired consistency (or purée in a blender or food
processor for younger baby).

1 adult and 1 child serving

/ / /

Semolina Primavera

1 large onion, chopped
1 clove garlic, minced
1 tbsp. butter, or 2 tbsp. peanut
   or olive oil
1½ cups homemade chicken
   stock (see page 281)
1 red or green sweet pepper,
   diced

1 tbsp. chopped fresh basil or
   oregano (or 1 tsp. dried)
1 zucchini, diced
1 large or 2 small ripe
   tomatoes, peeled and
   chopped
1 cup semolina (couscous)
2 tbsp. minced fresh parsley
3 tbsp. grated Parmesan cheese

In a large pot sauté onion and garlic in butter or oil until tender.
Add chicken stock, pepper, and basil or oregano, cover, and simmer for 5 minutes. Then add zucchini and simmer for 3 minutes
more, stirring occasionally. Add tomatoes and semolina and stir for
1 minute until semolina is thoroughly moistened. Cover tightly and

remove from heat. Let stand for 5 minutes, then fluff lightly with a fork. Sprinkle with parsley and Parmesan cheese before serving.

Serves 6

/ / /

Spinach and Potato Casserole

4 medium-size potatoes, peeled and sliced

4 eggs, beaten

¼ lb. (1 stick) butter, melted

2 cups grated cheddar or Swiss cheese

Two 10-oz. packages frozen chopped spinach, cooked and drained

In an oiled ovenproof dish make a layer of half the potato slices. Combine the eggs, melted butter, and grated cheese, and pour half the mixture over potatoes. Follow with a layer of spinach, making sure it is well drained. Add another layer of potatoes and cover with the rest of the egg, cheese, and butter mixture. Cover and bake in preheated 350° oven for 1¼ hours.

Serves 4 to 6

/ / /

Spanakopita
(Spinach and cheese in a flaky dough)

5 bunches fresh spinach, washed, stems removed, and finely chopped

4 eggs, lightly beaten

8 oz. feta cheese, crumbled

4 oz. Parmesan cheese, grated

1 onion, peeled, chopped, and sautéed

1 clove garlic

1 tsp. oregano

¼ lb. (1 stick) butter, melted

1 package phyllo dough (fresh or frozen)

Grease a lasagne pan and preheat oven to 350°. Mix spinach with eggs, feta cheese, Parmesan cheese, sautéed onion, garlic, and oregano. Very quickly brush a sheet of phyllo dough with melted butter and place in lasagne pan; repeat until you have a total of 10 sheets of dough in the pan. Fill pan with the spinach mixture, spreading it evenly over the dough, then cover with 7 more sheets of phyllo, each also brushed with melted butter. (If the sheets are larger than the pan, fold under at the edges.) Bake at 350° for 30 to 45 minutes until pastry is golden. Let stand a few minutes before cutting.

Serves 8 to 10

/ / /

Spinach Yogurt Bake

1 lb. fresh spinach, washed, or
   10 oz. package frozen
   chopped spinach
2 tbsp. butter

1 small onion, peeled and
   chopped
2 tbsp. flour
1 cup plain yogurt
1 cup grated jack cheese

Cook fresh spinach in covered pot, using just water left on leaves, for 3 minutes, stirring occasionally. (Cook frozen spinach according to package directions.) Drain well. Heat butter in a skillet and sauté onion in it until soft. Add flour and stir over medium heat for 1 minute. Gradually whisk in yogurt and mix well, followed by spinach, which should be stirred to coat with yogurt and onion, and heat through. Remove from heat and blend in grated cheese until melted. Pour mixture into greased 8x4 loaf pan and bake in preheated 350° oven for 20 minutes.

Serves 2

/ / /

Cheesy Baked Squash

1 summer squash	¼ cup olive oil
1 small zucchini	1 clove garlic, peeled and
1 yellow crookneck squash	mashed
5 mushrooms	¼ tsp. each oregano and basil
½ onion, peeled	½ cup grated jack cheese
1 red pepper, seeded	½ cup grated Parmesan cheese

Wash and slice all vegetables and steam together until tender. Meanwhile, combine olive oil, garlic, oregano, and basil. Transfer vegetables to an ovenproof casserole and cover with olive-oil mixture and then with the grated cheeses. Cover and bake in preheated 350° oven for 20 minutes. Remove cover and bake for another 10 minutes.

Serves 4

/ / /

Squash with Green Beans

1 young acorn squash, halved	3 tbsp. butter
and seeded	2 tbsp. grated Parmesan cheese
½ cup green beans, washed	1 tsp. finely chopped parsley
and trimmed	

Dot each squash half with 1 tablespoon butter and bake in preheated 375° oven for 20 minutes, or until tender. Meanwhile, steam green beans until tender, then cut into ½-inch pieces; toss with remaining 2 tablespoons butter. Fill both halves of squash with beans, top with Parmesan cheese, and sprinkle with parsley.

Serves 2

/ / /

Summer Salad

½ cup plain yogurt
½ cup mayonnaise
½ cup diced steamed green
  beans
½ cup diced cooked potato
½ cup diced steamed carrot

½ cup diced cooked beet
½ cup cucumber, peeled and
  diced
½ cup diced fresh or canned
  pineapple
4 hard-boiled eggs, diced

In a large bowl blend yogurt and mayonnaise well, then add all
other ingredients. Mix together gently until coated and refrigerate
until ready to serve.

Serves 6

/ / /

Sweet Potato and Apple Purée

1 small sweet potato or yam, peeled and sliced
½ apple, peeled, cored, and sliced
2 tbsp. milk
½ tsp. butter

Steam sweet potato and apple slices until tender. Purée or mash to
desired consistency with butter and milk.

2 or 3 child servings

/ / /

Sweet Potato Scramble

3 tbsp. butter
1 sweet potato (or yam),
   cooked and sliced

1 egg, beaten
1 tbsp. shredded jack cheese
½ tsp. chopped parsley

Melt 2 tablespoons butter in a skillet and sauté sweet potato slices in it until golden brown. In a small pan melt remaining butter and scramble egg over low heat, adding jack cheese and stirring until cheese is melted. Put sweet potato slices on a warm plate, cover with egg mixture, sprinkle with parsley, and serve immediately.

1 adult and 1 child serving

/ / /

Broiled Tomato

1 firm medium-size tomato
1 tbsp. chopped parsley
1 tsp. bread crumbs (or grated
  Parmesan cheese)

¼ tsp. lemon juice (optional)
1 tsp. butter

Wash tomato and cut in half. Sprinkle with parsley, bread crumbs, and lemon juice (if desired). Dot with butter and pop under pre-heated broiler for 5 minutes. Cut up 1 tomato half to serve to a child.

Serves 2

/ / /

Stuffed Tomato Treat

1 small firm tomato, washed
1 tbsp. butter
1 egg

1 tbsp. shredded Swiss or jack
   cheese
½ tsp. chopped parsley

Cut top off tomato, scoop out pulp and save, but discard hard core and seeds. Melt butter in a small skillet and scramble egg in it with tomato pulp. Fill tomato with mixture, top with shredded cheese, and place in a small pan with water to cover bottom. Bake for 15 to 20 minutes in preheated 350° oven until tomato is soft and cheese is melted. Sprinkle with parsley and serve.

1 child serving

/ / /

Tomato Eggplant Cups

¼ cup diced steamed eggplant
¼ cup cooked rice
2 firm medium-size tomatoes,
   washed

1 tsp. grated Parmesan cheese
1 tsp. finely chopped parsley
1 tsp. bread crumbs

Purée eggplant in a blender or food processor and mix with cooked rice. Cut top off tomatoes and scoop out cores and pulp. Discard cores, add pulp to eggplant and rice, and spoon mixture into tomato shells. Combine Parmesan cheese with parsley and bread crumbs, and spoon on top of eggplant filling. Place in a greased ovenproof dish and bake in a preheated 350° oven for 15 to 20 minutes, or until tomatoes are tender.

Serves 2

/ / /

Creamy Turnip

1 turnip, peeled and cut into
   small pieces
1 egg yolk

2 tbsp. cream (or half-and-
   half)
1 tbsp. butter
¼ tsp. grated lemon rind

Steam turnip until very soft. Mash well with all other ingredients, or purée to desired consistency. This method also works well with parsnips or rutabagas.

2 or 3 child servings

/ / /

Vegetable Custard

2 egg yolks
¼ cup milk
¼ cup puréed vegetables (carrots, peas, sweet potato, etc.)

Beat egg yolks and mix with milk and puréed vegetables. Pour into 2 buttered custard cups and bake in preheated 350° oven until set.

2 child servings

/ / /

Vegetable Rice Casserole

1 small cauliflower, trimmed
   and cut into flowerets
2 medium-size carrots, scrubbed
   and sliced
1 stalk celery, washed and
   sliced

4 tbsp. peanut or vegetable oil
1 cup rice, rinsed
5 cups chicken or vegetable
   stock (see page 281 or page
   282)
1 tbsp. chopped parsley

Sauté cauliflower, carrots, and celery in oil over low flame for 5 minutes, stirring to prevent sticking. Add rice and sauté for 2 more minutes. Grease a 2-quart ovenproof dish, add vegetables and rice, and pour stock over mixture. Cover and bake in preheated 375° oven for approximately 1 hour until rice and vegetables are tender. Sprinkle with parsley.

   For children, mash or purée to desired consistency.

Serves 4

/ / /

Yam and Carrot Balls with Raisins

¼ cup raisins
½ cup orange juice
1 medium-size yam or sweet
   potato, peeled and sliced
2 medium-size carrots, scrubbed
   and sliced

¼ small onion, peeled and
   chopped
1 tbsp. olive oil
1 tsp. grated orange rind
½ tsp. grated lemon rind
Chopped parsley

Soak raisins in orange juice while steaming yam and carrots. Sauté onion in the oil until tender and drain. When yam and carrots are tender, mash with a little of the orange juice, drain the raisins, and add along with all other ingredients except parsley to mashed vegetables. The mixture should be firm enough to hold together. Using a tablespoon, make little balls and place in a well-greased ovenproof casserole. Bake in preheated 375° oven for 20 minutes. Sprinkle with parsley before serving.

1 adult and 1 child serving

/ / /

Stuffed Zucchini with Apricot

1 large zucchini
2 tbsp. vegetable oil
½ onion, peeled and chopped
⅓ cup long-grained or basmati rice
1 medium-size tomato, peeled and chopped

1 cup vegetable or chicken stock (see page 282 or page 281)
⅓ cup diced cooked apricots, with juice
1 tsp. lemon juice

Halve the zucchini lengthwise and scrape out pulp (but save), leaving shell approximately ¾ inch thick. Boil shells in water to cover for 3 minutes and drain well. Heat oil in a large skillet and in it sauté onion and zucchini pulp until tender. Add rice, tomato, and broth, bring to a boil, cover, and cook for 15 minutes over low heat. Place half the apricots in an ovenproof dish with 4 tablespoons of their juice, add zucchini shells filled with the rice-zucchini mixture, and top with remainder of apricots. Sprinkle with lemon juice and bake in preheated 350° oven for 30 minutes, basting frequently with pan juices.

Purée serving for infants in blender.

Serves 2

/ / /

Zucchini Mushroom Pie

12 mushrooms, washed and
   sliced
4 green onions, washed and
   sliced
1 tbsp. butter
4 zucchini, washed and grated

1 cup grated cheddar or jack
   cheese
½ cup grated Parmesan cheese
½ cup wheat germ or bread
   crumbs
3 eggs, beaten
½ tsp. oregano

Sauté mushrooms and onions in butter until tender. Mix with zucchini, grated cheeses, wheat germ or bread crumbs, eggs, and oregano. Press mixture into an 8- or 9-inch greased pie dish and bake in preheated 350° oven for 35 minutes.

Serves 6 to 8

LEGUMES

Bean and Cheese Melt

1 cup mushrooms, washed and
   sliced
2 leeks, washed and sliced
2 tbsp. olive oil
1 tsp. oregano
Herb salt to taste (optional)

2 cups cooked white beans (see
   page 146)
6 tomatoes, peeled and sliced
1 cup grated Swiss or jack
   cheese

Sauté mushrooms and leeks in oil until tender, for 2 to 3 minutes, and season. Put beans in an ovenproof dish, add layer of sautéed vegetables and the tomatoes, and top with grated cheese and herb salt, if desired. Bake in preheated 325° oven for 15 minutes, or until cheese is bubbly.

Serves 4

/ / /

Cuban Black Beans

1½ cups cooked black beans
  (see page 146)
¼ cup bean cooking liquid
1 cup chopped seeded green
  peppers

1 cup chopped onions
2 tbsp. vegetable oil
1 bay leaf

Place beans in pan with their cooking liquid and heat gently. Sauté peppers and onions in vegetable oil for 5 minutes, or until tender. Drain any excess oil and add mixture to beans with the bay leaf. Continue to simmer for another 5 minutes, stirring occasionally. Remove bay leaf before serving.

Serves 4

/ / /

Peruvian Bean Purée

1 tbsp. chopped onion
1 tbsp. butter
¼ cup cooked lima beans
1 tbsp. chopped parsley

Sauté onion in butter until tender. Mash together with cooked lima beans, add parsley, and serve. May be puréed, if desired.

2 child servings

/ / /

Black-eyed Peas and Rice

16-oz. can black-eyed peas, or
  1 cup dried black-eyed peas,
  freshly cooked (see page
  146)
Water
½ cup rice

½ cup chopped onions
1 tsp. garlic salt
⅛ tsp. chili powder
1 cup shredded cheddar cheese

Drain peas, reserving liquid. Add water to liquid until it measures 2½ cups. In a large skillet combine black-eyed peas, rice, onions, garlic salt, chili powder, and liquid. Stir, bring to a boil, cover, reduce heat, and simmer for 20 minutes. Remove from heat. Sprinkle with grated cheese, replace cover, and let stand until cheese is melted and all liquid has been absorbed, about 5 minutes.

Serves 3 to 4

/ / /

Mild Vegetarian Chili with Beans

1 onion, peeled and chopped
2 tbsp. vegetable oil
3 tomatoes, peeled and chopped
½ cup tomato paste
½ tsp. basil
1 cup stock (from beans)

¼ tsp. oregano
¼ tsp. cumin
¼ tsp. garlic powder
1 cup pinto beans, cooked (see
  page 146)

Sauté onion in heated oil until golden, add all other ingredients except the beans, heat through, stirring well to blend flavors. Combine ingredients with pinto beans and simmer for 20 minutes before serving.

Serves 2

/ / /

Garbanzo Bean Purée

½ cup cooked garbanzo beans
   (see page 146)
¼ cup tahini (sesame-seed
   paste)
¼ cup lemon juice

1 tbsp. olive oil
1 clove garlic, mashed
½ tsp. paprika
1 tbsp. minced parsley

Put all ingredients except paprika and parsley into a blender or food processor, and purée. Garnish with parsley and paprika. May be served as a dip with sliced carrots, celery, cauliflower, etc., or spread on crackers or pita bread.

Makes about ¾ cup

/ / /

Lentil and Banana Mash

2 tbsp. cooked lentils (see page 148)
⅓ banana

Warm lentils, mash bananas, and combine ingredients. Purée for younger infants.

1 child serving

/ / /

Lentils Indian Style

1 cup lentils
1 tbsp. peanut or safflower oil
1 tsp. mustard seeds
1 clove garlic, crushed
¼ onion, peeled and chopped
¼ tsp. ground ginger

¼ tsp. garam masala (see page
  153)
½ cup tomato purée
4 pita breads (see page 254)
Grated cheddar cheese

Cook lentils (see page 148) until tender in a large pot. Drain. Heat oil in a skillet and cook mustard seeds in it until they pop. Add garlic and onion and sauté until golden. Add remaining ingredients, stir well, and cook for a few minutes. Add lentils and continue cooking for another 15 minutes.

For older children and adults, put 1 to 2 tbsp. of grated cheddar cheese inside pita bread and heat in oven until cheese is melted. Serve immediately with lentils.

Serves 4

/ / /

Lentil and Potato Stew

2 tbsp. lentils
½ potato, peeled and diced
1⅓ cups water
1 ripe tomato, peeled and
  chopped

¼ tsp. thyme
½ tsp. lemon juice
1 tsp. finely chopped parsley

Rinse lentils and put in a saucepan with potato and water. Bring to a boil, reduce heat, and simmer, covered, for 20 minutes. Add tomato and thyme, stir, and cook for another 5 to 10 minutes, still covered, over low heat. Add lemon juice, sprinkle with parsley, and serve.

2 or 3 child servings

/ / /

Lentil Roast

2 tbsp. cooked lentils (see
   page 148)
1 small potato, cooked and
   mashed

¼ cup cooked peas
2 egg yolks, beaten
3 tbsp. grated cheddar cheese

Grease an ovenproof dish, mix first four ingredients, and place in dish. Top with grated cheese and bake in preheated 325° oven for 30 minutes.

1 adult and 1 child serving

/ / /

Lentils with Tomato and Celery

½ onion, peeled and chopped
1 clove garlic, peeled and
   mashed
2 stalks celery, washed and
   finely chopped
1 tbs. vegetable oil

¼ cup reserved lentil cooking
   liquid
1 cup cooked lentils, (see
   page 148)
2 tomatoes, peeled and chopped

Sauté onion, garlic, and celery in oil until tender and drain. Add reserved liquid to lentils and heat through gently. Add sautéed vegetables and tomatoes to lentils and simmer over low heat for 5 minutes, stirring occasionally.

Serves 4

/ / /

Lima Beans

1 cup small dried lima beans,
   washed
2½ cups water
1 tbsp. safflower oil
1 onion, peeled and finely
   chopped

2 tomatoes, peeled, chopped,
   and sautéed
1 tsp. minced parsley
Dash marjoram
1 tsp. vegetable salt (optional)
Dash white pepper (optional)

In a heavy pot place lima beans and water, bring to a boil, and cook over high heat for 2 minutes. Remove from heat and let stand for 1 hour. Then stir in oil, return to a boil, reduce heat, and simmer for 45 minutes. In the last 5 minutes, add onion, tomatoes, parsley, marjoram, and salt and pepper, if desired.

Serves 6

/ / /

Frijoles I
(Refried Beans)

1 cup dried pinto beans, cooked
   (see page 146) and puréed
1 small clove garlic, mashed
¼ cup grated onion

⅓ cup grated cheddar cheese
1 tsp. tamari or soy sauce
Pinch each basil and oregano

Mix all ingredients together and heat in a double boiler until cheese is melted and blended.

Serves 4

/ / /

Frijoles II

1 cup dried pinto beans, cooked (see page 146)
¼ cup vegetable oil
½ cup grated cheddar or jack cheese

Stir oil into cooked and heated beans and mash. Add grated cheese and continue to cook until cheese is completely melted.

Serves 4

/ / /

Frijoles III

¼ cup corn oil
1 cup dried pinto beans, cooked (see page 146)
½ cup tomatoes, peeled and diced

¼ cup chopped onion
1 cup queso fresco cheese, crumbled

Heat oil in a skillet and add beans with a slotted spoon. Mash with a potato masher. Add water or broth, if necessary, to bring to desired consistency, stir in tomatoes and onion, and cook until onion is tender. Serve in individual bowls, topped with crumbled cheese.

Serves 4

/ / /

Soy Potato Burgers

1 cup dried soybeans, cooked
  (see page 146)
2 raw potatoes, peeled and
  grated
1 onion, finely chopped

6 tbsp. chopped hazelnuts
2 tbsp. milk
¼ tsp. salt
Vegetable oil for frying

Grind soybeans and hazelnuts in a blender or food processor, and combine with all other ingredients except oil. Make into small thin patties and sauté in a little oil over low heat until potatoes and onion are cooked through.

Serves 4

/ / /

Mini Tostadas

1 can vegetarian refried beans, or 1½ cups homemade (see page 178)
2 tomatoes, finely chopped
1 cup grated cheddar cheese
Package small tortillas

Warm 6 tortillas in the oven according to directions on package. Gently heat the beans and spread a spoonful on each tortilla. Cover each with chopped tomato and sprinkle with grated cheese. Pop under preheated broiler for 2 or 3 minutes, or just until cheese is melted.

For older children and adults, shredded cooked chicken or cooked ground beef may be added, topped with olives and hot sauce.

Makes 6 tostadas

/ / /

Small White Beans

1 cup dried white beans,
   cooked
1 onion, peeled and chopped
2 tbsp. vegetable oil

¼ cup reserved bean liquid
1 tomato, peeled and chopped
1 tbsp. chopped parsley

Cook beans until tender (see page 147) in a saucepan. Sauté onion in oil until tender and drain. Add onion and all other ingredients to beans, and simmer for a few minutes to develop flavor, stirring to prevent sticking.

Serves 4

TOFU

Tofu and Cauliflower

2 oz. mashed tofu (approximately ¼ cup)
2 small cauliflowerets
1 tbsp. shredded cheddar cheese

Steam cauliflowerets for 10 minutes and mash together with tofu. Place mixture in a small heatproof dish, top with shredded cheese, and pop under preheated broiler until the cheese is melted.

1 child serving

/ / /

Tofu-Cheese Soufflé

1½ slices whole wheat bread
1 tbsp. butter
3 oz. sharp cheddar cheese,
    grated
1 tbsp. chopped onion

3 oz. tofu, cut into ½-inch
    slices
¾ cup milk
2 eggs, beaten

Butter an ovenproof casserole. Spread bread with butter, break into several small pieces, and cover bottom of casserole with it. Then add grated cheese in one layer, the onion, and lastly the tofu. Combine milk and eggs, pour into casserole, and let stand for 1 hour. Preheat oven to 350°, place casserole in a larger pan of water, and bake for 45 minutes.

Serves 2 to 3

/ / /

Tofu with Egg

2 tsp. butter
1 oz. tofu (2 tbsp.)
2 egg yolks
1 tsp. milk

In a skillet melt the butter, add tofu and mash, then sauté over medium heat until lightly brown. Beat egg yolks and milk together well, add to tofu, and scramble until eggs are cooked.

1 child serving

/ / /

Fried Tofu with Mushrooms

1 tbsp. peanut oil
1 tbsp. chopped onion
3 mushrooms, washed and
    sliced

2 tbsp. cooked peas
3 oz. tofu, cubed

Heat oil in a skillet and sauté onion in it until golden. Add mushrooms, peas, and tofu. Cook for 5 minutes over medium heat, stirring to brown tofu on all sides.

1 adult and 1 child serving

/ / /

Mushroom Tofu Stroganoff

16 oz. tofu
1 tbsp. vegetable oil
1 clove garlic, minced
¾ lb. mushrooms, washed and
    sliced

¾ cup chicken stock (see
    page 281)
½ tsp. basil
Dash pepper
8 oz. plain yogurt
2 tbsp. flour

Drain tofu on paper towels and cut into ½-inch cubes. Heat oil in a skillet and fry tofu in it for 3 or 4 minutes, stirring to prevent sticking. Add garlic and mushrooms and cook for another 2 or 3 minutes until mushrooms are tender. Remove tofu and mushrooms, add chicken stock, basil, and pepper to skillet, and bring to a boil. Mix yogurt with flour and stir into stock, cooking until mixture bubbles. Cook for 1 minute more, then stir in tofu and mushrooms and heat through. Serve with noodles.

Serves 4

/ / /

Tofu-Rice Casserole

4 tsp. vegetable oil	12 oz. tofu, cut up
2 tbsp. butter	1 cup milk
1 medium onion, thinly sliced	½ cup bread crumbs
1 cup cooked rice	2 oz. cheddar cheese, grated

Heat half the oil in a large skillet and add the butter. When melted, sauté onion until soft, then add rice and sauté for 2 minutes more. Gently stir in tofu, and sauté for another 2 minutes. Use remaining oil to grease an ovenproof dish, fill with tofu-rice mixture, and pour the cup of milk over it. Mix bread crumbs and grated cheese, sprinkle over the dish, and pop under preheated broiler at medium temperature for 10 minutes, or until cheese is melted.

Serves 2 to 3

/ / /

Vegetables Tofu

1 small sweet potato, peeled and cubed
1 small carrot, scrubbed and sliced
1 tbsp. butter
2 oz. tofu

Steam sweet potato and carrot together until tender. Mash well with butter and tofu. Serve immediately.

1 adult and 1 child serving

CHEESE AND EGGS

Cheese Enchiladas

Enchilada Sauce (see below)
Vegetable oil
1 package corn tortillas (12 tortillas)

4 oz. shredded cheddar cheese
4 oz. shredded jack cheese
Toothpicks
1 green onion, chopped

Make enchilada sauce. Heat oil in a frying pan and cook tortillas on both sides for a few minutes until soft. Drain on paper towels. Dip tortillas in enchilada sauce, lay on flat surface, and fill with 1 tablespoon each cheddar and jack cheeses. Roll tortillas carefully and pin with toothpick. Lay enchiladas side by side in a large oven-proof dish, cover with remaining sauce, and sprinkle with chopped onion and rest of cheese. Bake in preheated 350° oven for 10 to 15 minutes until cheese is melted. Serve immediately.

ENCHILADA SAUCE:

1 cup tomato sauce (see page 283) or 8-oz. can tomato sauce
3 medium-size tomatoes, peeled and chopped

1 onion, peeled and chopped
4-oz. can diced mild green chiles
½ bunch fresh cilantro, washed and trimmed

Mix all ingredients in blender or food processor and pour into container large enough to dip tortillas.

Serves 6 to 8

/ / /

Cheese and Lentil Loaf

½ lb. shredded cheddar cheese
2 cups cooked drained lentils
  (see page 148)
½ small onion, peeled and
  chopped
⅛ tsp. black pepper
¼ tsp. thyme

1 cup, packed, soft bread
  crumbs
1 egg, lightly beaten
1 tbsp. butter, melted
1 cup tomato sauce (see
  page 283)

Blend together shredded cheese, lentils, and onion, and add pepper and thyme. Sitr in bread crumbs, beaten egg, and butter, and mix all ingredients thoroughly. Grease a loaf pan well, add mixture, and bake in preheated 325° oven for 45 minutes. Serve with heated tomato sauce.

Serves 4

/ / /

Cottage Cheese Delight

1 cup cottage cheese
½ cup milk
2 cups grated jack cheese

3 eggs, lightly beaten
¼ cup melted butter
½ cup all-purpose flour

Mix all ingredients in a large bowl, adding flour last, and beat until smooth. Pour mixture into a buttered ovenproof dish and bake in preheated 375° oven for 40 minutes, or until the dish is set and golden in color.

Serves 4

/ / /

Cottage Cheese with Scrambled Egg

1 tbsp. cottage cheese*
1 egg
1 tsp. butter

Mix cottage cheese and egg in a bowl and beat well. Melt butter in a skillet and pour in mixture. Scramble over medium-low heat until cooked through.

1 child serving

*Two tablespoons of rice may be substituted for cottage cheese, if desired.

/ / /

Quesadilla
(Tortilla with Cheese)

1 small Mexican flour tortilla (see page 253)
2 tbsp. grated jack or cheddar cheese

Spread grated cheese on half the tortilla, fold, and press down. Place on a baking sheet or foil in preheated 325° oven until cheese is melted.

Adults may add jalapeño peppers, *salsa*, guacamole, and sour cream, if desired.

1 child serving

/ / /

Ricotta Cheese Pancakes

3 eggs
1 cup ricotta or cottage cheese
2 tbsp. vegetable oil

2 tbsp. wheat germ
2 tbsp. flour

Combine all ingredients in a blender or food processor and mix until smooth. Pour 3-inch to 4-inch rounds of batter onto a greased and preheated griddle. Cook until bubbles form, turn, and continue to cook until brown.

Serves 4

/ / /

Asparagus Omelet

1 tbsp. butter
4 eggs, beaten
½ cup Swiss or Jarlsberg
    cheese, cut into small cubes

¾ cup cooked asparagus, cut
    into small pieces
½ cup tomatoes, peeled and
    cut up

Melt butter in an omelet or frying pan until bubbling. Pour eggs into pan and rotate until base is covered, pulling cooked egg gently inward and letting uncooked egg spread to the side. Add cheese, asparagus, and tomatoes and allow eggs to set. With a spatula, carefully fold omelet over, and cook for another minute or two, until cheese is melted. Slide omelet onto a warm plate and serve immediately.

Serves 2

/ / /

Egg Nest

½ cup puréed cooked fresh corn
1 tbsp. grated Parmesan cheese
1 egg

Put corn into a small individual ovenproof casserole and sprinkle with Parmesan cheese. Make a hollow in the corn and carefully break an egg into it. Bake in preheated 325° oven until set.

1 adult or older child serving

/ / /

Petite Omelet

1 tsp. butter
1 egg
1 oz. cooked chicken or ham, etc., cut into small cubes

1 small tomato, peeled and chopped
1 tsp. chopped parsley

Melt butter over medium heat in a small frying pan. Beat egg well in a bowl and mix in all other ingredients. When butter starts to bubble, pour egg mixture into center of pan and rotate to spread mixture, pulling cooked egg from sides and letting uncooked egg spread outside until omelet is set. Fold carefully with a spatula and slide onto a warm plate.

1 adult serving to share with 1 child

/ / /

Piselli con Uova
(Peas with Eggs)

2 tbsp. olive oil
1 small onion, peeled and
  chopped
2 cups canned plum tomatoes,
  puréed

½ tsp. basil
1 cup cooked fresh peas, or
  thawed frozen peas
4 eggs, individually beaten

In a large frying pan, heat oil and sauté onion in it until translu-
cent. Add puréed tomatoes and basil, and simmer for 15 minutes,
stirring occasionally. Then add peas and simmer for another 10
minutes. Add 1 beaten egg to pan and cook for 1 minute, stirring
constantly. Do this 3 more times, allowing 1 minute for each egg to
cook before adding the next. Serve immediately.

Serves 2

/ / /

Poached Egg with Spinach

1 bunch spinach (¾ to 1 lb.), washed and stems removed
2 eggs
6 orange segments, peeled and seeded

Cook spinach in a tightly covered pan, using only water remaining
on the leaves, until tender. Remove from pan and chop fine. Poach
eggs until whites are firm and place on beds of spinach in 2 bowls.
Decorate around eggs with orange segments.

1 adult and 1 child serving

/ / /

Scrambled Eggs with Peppers

1 tbsp. olive oil
1 medium-size onion, peeled
   and chopped
1 clove garlic, minced

1 medium-size bell pepper,
   washed, seeded, and diced
3 eggs, beaten

Heat oil in a skillet and in it gently sauté onion, garlic, and pepper until tender, about 10 minutes. Add beaten eggs and scramble over medium-low heat together with vegetables until firm. Serve with whole wheat bread.

1 adult and 1 child serving

FISH

Haddock with Egg Butter

1 lb. fresh filleted haddock
Milk to cover
4 tbsp. butter
1 egg, hard-boiled and finely chopped

Place haddock in a saucepan, cover fish with milk, and put a lid on pan. Slowly bring milk to a boil, reduce heat immediately, then simmer gently for 12 to 15 minutes. Meanwhile, melt butter in a small saucepan, add chopped egg, and mix. Remove fish from saucepan with a slotted spoon, place on a hot platter, and cover with egg-butter mixture. Serve immediately with steamed carrots and potatoes.

Serves 3 to 4

/ / /

Baked Haddock and Potatoes

3 large potatoes, scrubbed and
   sliced ⅛ inch thick
¼ cup melted butter
1 package frozen haddock
   (about 1 lb.), partially
   thawed

Juice of ½ lemon
½ tsp. paprika
½ tsp. dill

Generously grease an ovenproof casserole, add a layer of half the potato slices, and pour a little butter over them. Layer fish over potatoes, and sprinkle with lemon juice and half the paprika and dill. Top with remaining potatoes, cover with remaining butter, paprika, and dill. Cover and bake in preheated 375° oven for 1 hour, removing cover during the last 15 minutes and basting with butter from the casserole.

Serves 3 to 4

/ / /

Fish with Fresh Tomato

One 4-oz. piece of skinned and filleted cod, halibut, or West Coast
   orange roughy
1 small ripe tomato
1 tsp. finely chopped parsley

Place fish in a saucepan of boiling water and simmer for 10 minutes, or until opaque. Remove with a slotted spoon and drain. Add tomato to boiling water for 2 minutes, then remove from water, peel, and chop well. Sprinkle fish with tomato and parsley, and serve with mashed potatoes.

1 adult and 1 child serving

/ / /

Oven-Baked Fish

1 small fillet of fish (about 4 oz.), skinned	*¼ cup milk*
1 egg	*⅛ tsp. dill*
	½ tsp. chopped parsley

Cut fish into small pieces and place in a lightly oiled ovenproof dish. Beat together egg, milk, dill, and parsley, and pour over fish. Bake in preheated 350° oven for 30 minutes, or until fish flakes easily and is white in color.

Serve with baked sweet potato and peas.

1 adult and 1 child serving

/ / /

Fish and Rice Casserole

1½ cups rice (quick-cooking or basmati)	*1 lb. fresh sole, sea bass, or West Coast orange roughy, filleted*
1 cup shredded carrot	*Juice of ½ lemon*
⅓ cup thinly sliced celery	*Paprika*
2 tbsp. butter	
Grated peel of 1 lemon	
1½ cups boiling chicken stock (preferably homemade, page 281)	

In a 12 × 8 baking dish, combine rice, carrot, celery, 1 tablespoon butter, lemon peel, and boiling chicken stock. Cover with foil and bake in preheated 400° oven for 5 minutes. Remove from oven and stir. Arrange fish on top of rice, sprinkle with lemon juice and paprika, and dot with remaining tablespoon of butter. Bake, covered, for 25 minutes, or until fish flakes easily with fork.

Serves 4

/ / /

Simple Fish and Vegetables

2 oz. cod fillet, skinned
1 small carrot, scrubbed and thinly sliced
2 tbsp. chopped celery

Put fish, carrot, and celery in a small pan, and add enough boiling water to cover. Simmer for 10 to 15 minutes, or until fish and vegetables are cooked through. Pour off water, leaving just enough to mash with the fish and vegetables. Serve with rice.

1 child serving

/ / /

Fiske Kaker
(Norwegian Fish Cakes)

1 lb. fresh haddock or cod, skinned, boned, and cut into pieces
1 tbsp. potato flour or cornstarch

1½ tsp. salt (necessary for the right texture)
⅛ tsp. ground nutmeg
1 cup milk
4 tbsp. butter

Put fish, flour, salt, and nutmeg in a food processor fitted with metal blade. Process until fish has become a coarse purée, scraping down sides with spatula as necessary. With processor running, add milk, 1 tablespoonful at a time, until ½ cup has been used. Then increase quantity to 2 or 3 tablespoonsful at a time until all milk has been used. Melt 2 tablespoons of butter in a frying pan over medium heat. Have ready a bowl of water and a tablespoon. Moisten hand, dip tablespoon into water, then into fish purée; with hand and spoon form a round ball. Place fish cake in a frying pan and flatten with a spatula or spoon until it is about ¾ inch thick. Fry until brown, turn, and repeat on the other side until fish cake is cooked through. Repeat until all purée is used up, adding remaining butter as needed for frying.

Serves 4

/ / /

Fiskepudding
(Norwegian Fish Pudding)

1½ tbsp. soft butter	*2 eggs*
2 tbsp. fine bread crumbs	*1 tsp. salt*
2 tbsp. cornstarch	*⅛ tsp. nutmeg*
1 cup milk	*⅛ tsp. white pepper*
1 cup whipping cream	*1 tbsp. freshly chopped parsley*
1 lb. fresh cod or haddock, skinned, boned, and cut into pieces	

Butter a small loaf pan, using ½ tablespoon of the butter, sprinkle with bread crumbs, and set aside. Mix cornstarch with milk and bring to a boil in a small saucepan over medium heat. Stir constantly until mixture has consistency of medium-thick white sauce. Remove from heat and cool completely. Stir in cream.

Using metal blade, chop fish in a food processor, add eggs, 1 tablespoon butter, salt, nutmeg, and pepper, and process until puréed. With machine still running, add cream sauce through feed tube and mix until well blended, scraping sides of bowl as necessary. Pour mixture into a greased loaf pan. Fill a larger pan with hot water to halfway when loaf pan is set inside it. Carefully place in preheated 325° oven and bake for 1 hour.

WHITE SAUCE:

1 tbsp. butter	1/4 cup milk
1 tbsp. flour	1 tsp. curry powder
Up to 1 cup fish, chicken, or vegetable stock	

Melt butter and stir in flour, using wire whisk, over low heat. Add a little of the broth, stirring constantly, and continue adding broth until sauce is completely smooth and of the desired consistency. It is important to add stock slowly, stirring constantly, and maintain low heat to prevent lumpiness. Add curry powder and let sauce simmer for 5 to 10 minutes. Add milk, stir, and simmer another minute. Serve fish pudding with sauce over it, garnished with parsley.

Serves 4 to 6

/ / /

Creamy Halibut Bake

4 medium-size fresh halibut steaks	2 tbsp. butter
1/2 tsp. dill	4 tomatoes, peeled and chopped
1 onion, peeled and chopped	1/2 cup cream (or half-and-half)
4 slices lemon	

Place halibut steaks side by side in an ovenproof casserole. Sprinkle with dill and onion. Place a slice of lemon on each steak, dot with butter, and cover with chopped tomatoes. Bake in preheated 375° oven, covered, for 30 minutes. Remove cover, add cream, and bake for another 10 minutes, basting occasionally.

Serves 4

/ / /

Poached Fish with Yogurt Sauce

2 lbs. firm white fish, filleted

1 quart water

1 small onion, peeled and
    quartered

6 whole black peppercorns

3 whole allspice

3 tbsp. lemon juice

1 bay leaf

1 tsp. salt

½ cup dry white wine

2 tbsp. chopped parsley

Yogurt Sauce (see below)

Place all ingredients except fish and parsley in a large skillet and bring to a boil. Reduce heat and simmer, uncovered, for 30 minutes over low heat until flavors are blended. Add fish, cover, and continue to simmer for 15 to 20 minutes until fish flakes easily when tested with a fork. Remove fish with a slotted spoon and drain well. Top with yogurt sauce. Garnish with parsley.

YOGURT SAUCE:

1 cup plain yogurt

1 tbsp. cornstarch

2 egg yolks

2 tbsp. lemon juice

⅓ cup mayonnaise

Mix yogurt with cornstarch in a small saucepan and bring to a low simmer, stirring with a wire whisk. Cook for 2 minutes, still stirring. Remove from heat. Beat together egg yolks and lemon juice and slowly pour into yogurt mixture. Stir well. When cool, stir in the mayonnaise.

Serves 4

/ / /

Baked Potatoes with Salmon Sauce

4 medium-size potatoes
4 tbsp. butter
3 green onions, white parts
    only, finely chopped
½ cup mushrooms, washed and
    sliced

¼ cup all-purpose flour
½ tsp. marjoram
⅛ tsp. white pepper
2 cups milk
16-oz. can salmon, drained
    (reserve liquid)

Scrub potatoes and bake in preheated 350° oven for 1 hour, or until done. Meanwhile, melt butter in a saucepan, add onions and mushrooms, and sauté until tender. Add flour, marjoram, and pepper, mix well, then add the reserved liquid from the salmon. Slowly pour in milk, stirring constantly to mix, and cook over low heat until sauce is smooth and thickened. Break salmon into bite-size pieces, add to sauce, and cook until thoroughly heated. Split open baked potatoes and spoon salmon sauce over them.

Serves 4

/ / /

Steamed Salmon Loaf

1 cup milk
1½ cups soft bread cubes
Two 16-oz. cans salmon with
    liquid

1 cup chopped celery
1 cup chopped onions
¼ cup chopped green pepper
4 eggs

2 tsp. grated lemon peel   ½ tsp. thyme
1 tsp. lemon juice   ½ tsp. black pepper
½ tsp. paprika

Scald milk, add bread cubes, and mix well. Flake salmon and add
it and liquid to milk. Add celery, onions, green pepper, eggs, lemon
peel and juice, paprika, thyme, and pepper to pan and mix well.
Oil an ovenproof loaf pan (about 9 × 5) and turn mixture into pan.
Set loaf pan in a larger pan half filled with hot water and bake in
preheated 325° oven for 1½ hours. For easier cutting, let the salmon
loaf sit for a while before serving.

Serves 6 to 8

/ / /

Salmon Soufflé

2 tbsp. butter   2 egg yolks, beaten
2 tbsp. flour   16-oz. can salmon, drained, or
1 cup milk   2 cups cooked salmon, flaked
½ tsp. salt   2 egg whites, stiffly beaten

Gently melt butter in a small saucepan, add flour, and mix. Add
milk and salt, and cook over low heat, stirring with a wooden spoon
until mixture is smooth. Remove from heat. Mix a little of the sauce
with the egg yolks, blend well, and return mixture to saucepan.
Add flaked salmon to sauce, then gently fold in stiffly beaten egg
whites. Pour into a well-greased soufflé dish and bake in preheated
325° oven for 45 minutes.

Serves 3 to 4

/ / /

Baked Sea Bass Oriental

1 whole sea bass, cleaned
1 onion, sliced
3 slices lemon
Spicy Sweet Sauce (see below)

Place fish in an ovenproof dish and cover with onion, lemon, and the sauce. Bake in preheated 350° oven for 30 to 45 minutes, or until fish separates from the bones easily.

Check carefully to make sure *all* bones are removed before serving to children.

SPICY SWEET SAUCE:

¼ cup soy sauce
3 small slices fresh ginger
½ tsp. chili powder

½ tsp. turmeric
½ tsp. sugar

Mix all ingredients together well before pouring over fish.

Serves 3 to 4

/ / /

Seafood Salad

8 oz. vermicelli
¾ cup celery, thinly sliced
¼ cup chopped green or red
  pepper
3 hard-boiled eggs, chopped

2-oz. jar pimientos, chopped
  (optional)
Dressing (see below)
12 oz. cooked shrimp, crab, or
  filleted fish

Break vermicelli into bite-size pieces and cook in boiling water until tender (about 7 or 8 minutes). Drain and cool. Just before serving, mix all ingredients together in a large bowl with the dressing, but leave fish until last. Toss well and serve immediately.

DRESSING:

½ cup mayonnaise
½ cup buttermilk
1½ tbsp. lime or lemon juice
1 tsp. mixed Italian herbs

This is best made in advance. Combine all ingredients, mix well, and chill slightly before using.

Serves 4

/ / /

Shrimp with Almond Yogurt Sauce

2 limes, thinly sliced
2 lb. medium shrimp, peeled, cleaned, and deveined
⅓ cup very thinly slivered almonds
3 tbsp. butter
2 tbsp. minced onion

1 small clove garlic, minced
1 tsp. all-purpose flour
6 tbsp. vegetable or chicken stock (see page 282 or page 281)
½ cup plain yogurt

Line the bottom of a shallow ovenproof dish with sliced limes and arrange shrimp over them. Sprinkle with 1 tablespoon slivered almonds and put under preheated broiler for 8 minutes, turning once after 5 minutes. Transfer to a serving platter and keep warm. Melt butter in a saucepan, add remaining almonds, onion, and garlic. Sauté until onion is golden, then stir in flour, add stock, and continue to cook over low to medium heat until sauce has thickened.

Remove from heat and stir in yogurt until creamy and well blended. Sauce may be served over shrimp or on the side.

Serves 4

/ / /

Shrimp and Okra Stew

3 tbsp. vegetable oil
1 medium-size onion, chopped
1 lb. fresh or frozen okra,
  sliced thin
4 medium-size tomatoes,
  blanched and peeled

2 ripe plantains (or bananas),
  cubed
½ lb. cooked shrimp
2 to 3 cups broth (chicken, fish,
  or vegetable)
Juice of a lime (or lemon)

Heat oil in a large pot, add onion, and sauté until glazed. Add okra, tomatoes, and plantains (or bananas). Simmer for 5 minutes, stirring occasionally, then add shrimp, broth, and lime (or lemon) juice. Bring stew to a boil, immediately reduce heat, and simmer for 30 minutes, covered. Stir frequently but gently to prevent sticking.

A little salt or other seasonings, such as dill, garlic, pepper, etc., may be added for adults. Serve over rice.

Serves 4

/ / /

Sole Meunière

¼ tsp. salt
⅛ tsp. white pepper
¼ cup flour
1 lb. fresh fillet of sole

¼ pound (1 stick) butter,
  divided in half
2 tbsp. fresh lime or lemon
  juice
1 tbsp. finely chopped parsley

Combine salt and pepper with flour and coat fish lightly with the mixture. Melt half the butter in a frying pan until bubbly and sauté fish in it, carefully turning once when the first side is browned. Fish is cooked when white and flaky. Remove to a hot platter.

Clean pan, add remaining butter and lime juice and parsley, and heat gently until butter is melted and ingredients are mixed. Remove from heat and pour over fish. Serve immediately.

Serves 3 to 4

/ / /

Calamari

3 tbsp. olive or safflower oil
2 large cloves garlic, crushed
1 onion, peeled and sliced thin
1 stalk celery, chopped
12 mushrooms, washed and
   sliced

2 tomatoes, peeled and chopped
1½ cups tomato sauce (see
   page 283)
1 tsp. tarragon
1 lb. squid, cleaned and cut up

Heat oil in a large pan and in it cook garlic, onion, and celery until tender. Add mushrooms, tomatoes, tomato sauce, and tarragon, and continue cooking over medium heat for 10 minutes, stirring occasionally to prevent sticking. Add squid to sauce, mix well, and bring mixture to a boil. Reduce heat immediately and simmer for 10 minutes. (Important: Do not overcook squid, as it will become tough.) Serve with rice and a green salad.

Serves 4

/ / /

Stir-Fried Squid with Snow Peas

FOR MARINADE:

½-inch piece fresh ginger,
  peeled and grated

Juice of 1 lime
1 tbsp. soy sauce

1 lb. squid, cleaned and cut
  up*
6 tbsp. peanut oil
24 Chinese snow peas, washed
  and trimmed

12 mushrooms, washed and
  sliced
½ tsp. arrowroot

Combine ingredients for marinade, cut squid into 1- × ½-inch pieces, and marinate for 15 minutes. Heat oil in a wok or heavy frying pan until very hot, and add squid, snow peas, and mushrooms. Stir-fry for approximately 3 minutes until squid is opaque and snow peas are bright green. Remove from wok to a heated plate. Add arrowroot to marinade, put in wok, and stir well until heated through to make a sauce. Pour over squid and serve immediately with rice.

Serves 3 to 4

*Abalone, sea bass, or halibut may be substituted for squid, if desired.

/ / /

Broiled Sturgeon

1 lb. sturgeon, skinned and
  boned
3 tbsp. olive oil

2 tbsp. lemon juice
2 tbsp. chopped fresh dill
Paprika

Cut fish into 1½-inch chunks and marinate in mixture of oil, lemon, and dill for 20 minutes. Drain fish and reserve marinade. Place fish in a shallow heatproof dish, sprinkle with paprika, and place under preheated broiler for 5 minutes, basting frequently with marinade. Turn and broil for 5 more minutes, continuing to baste. Fish is cooked when it becomes white and flaky.

Serves 3 to 4

/ / /

Tuna Fish Casserole

2 cups wide egg noodles
2 cups Cheese Sauce (see below)
Two 6½-oz. cans white or light tuna, drained and flaked

Cook noodles as directed on package. Meanwhile, make the cheese sauce. Preheat oven to 350° and mix noodles, tuna, and cheese sauce together in an ovenproof dish. Bake for 20 to 30 minutes.

CHEESE SAUCE:

3 tbsp. butter or margarine   *4 oz. medium-sharp cheddar*
3 tbsp. flour   *cheese, grated*
10 oz. milk   *Dash white pepper*

Melt butter or margarine over *very low heat* until melted. Add flour and stir gently with a wooden spoon. Add milk and bring slowly to a boil, stirring constantly to prevent lumpiness. Reduce heat and simmer for no more than 2 to 3 minutes. Add cheese and pepper, and continue stirring until cheese is melted.

Serves 3 to 4

POULTRY

Chicken Breasts with Lime Butter

4 boneless chicken breasts,
   skinned
1 egg, beaten
½ cup bread crumbs
2 tbsp. olive oil

Juice of 1 lime
¼ pound (1 stick) butter
1 tsp. minced fresh chives
½ tsp. dill

Place chicken breasts between two pieces of wax paper and pound until very thin. (A rolling pin or a wooden potato masher works well.) Dip chicken in beaten egg, then in bread crumbs. Heat oil in a skillet and sauté chicken in it over medium heat for 2 to 3 minutes on each side, or until meat is white throughout. Transfer to a warm platter. Drain remaining oil from skillet, add lime juice, and heat over low flame until it bubbles. Add butter and stir until mixture becomes opaque and thickened. Stir in chives and dill. Spoon sauce over chicken and serve immediately.

Serves 4

/ / /

Boned Chicken Chinese Style

1 boned chicken breast, sliced
   thin and cut into bite-size
   pieces

½ cup soy sauce
2 tbsp. port or sherry
1 slice lemon

2 cloves garlic, peeled and split
   in half
2 slices fresh ginger
1 tbsp. peanut or safflower oil
1 cup bean sprouts, washed

1 cup mushrooms, washed and
   sliced
1 onion, peeled and sliced
2 cups Chinese snow peas,
   washed and trimmed
1 tsp. cornstarch or arrowroot

Marinate chicken breast in mixture of soy sauce, port or sherry, lemon, garlic, and ginger for at least 1 hour. Drain chicken and save marinade. Heat oil in a wok over medium-high heat. Throw in sprouts, mushrooms, onion, and snow peas, and stir-fry for 2 to 3 minutes. Remove vegetables and add a little more oil, if necessary, to cook chicken. Stir-fry chicken for 5 to 7 minutes, or until cooked through. Remove chicken and set aside with vegetables. Mix cornstarch or arrowroot with marinade, first removing lemon, ginger, and garlic, and stir well. Throw chicken and vegetables back into wok, add marinade, and mix together over high heat. Serve immediately with rice.

Serves 2

/ / /

Cuban Chicken

1 onion, peeled and quartered
1 green pepper, washed,
   seeded, and quartered
1 chicken, washed and cut into
   serving pieces
1 small can tomato sauce
1 small jar green olives,
   drained
1 small jar pimientos, cut in
   1-inch squares

1 handful raisins
½ bottle Cuban or Californian
   white wine
1½ tbsp. cumin
1 tsp. garlic salt
4 potatoes, quartered
4 carrots, scrubbed and cut
   into thirds

Place onion and pepper in blender or food processor, using chopping blade, and chop fine. Put chicken pieces into a large pot, add onion, green pepper, and all other ingredients except potatoes and carrots. Bring to a boil, reduce heat, and simmer for 1½ hours. Add potatoes and carrots and return to heat for ½ hour more, or until vegetables are cooked through.

Serves 4

/ / /

Chicken Fricassee

1 whole stewing chicken	1 tsp. salt
1 carrot, scrubbed	½ tsp. white pepper
1 onion, peeled	White sauce (see page 284)
2 stalks celery, washed	3 tbsp. chopped parsley

Clean chicken well, put in a heavy pot, and cover with water. Add carrot, onion, celery, and salt and pepper. Bring to a boil, reduce heat, and simmer for 1 hour, or until chicken falls from the bones. Remove chicken from pot with tongs, let cool, then remove meat and discard skin and bones. Strain broth through a sieve, saving some to use for white sauce and discarding carrot, onion, and celery. Make white sauce according to recipe, using broth from the chicken. Cut chicken into bite-size pieces, add to white sauce, heat thoroughly, and pour fricassee into a heated serving dish. Dress with chopped parsley and serve with cauliflower, carrots, and buttered potatoes.

Serves 4

/ / /

Pineapple Chicken Supreme

1 chicken breast, boned,
   skinned, and pounded flat
2 tbsp. flour
¼ cup oil
¼ cup fresh or canned
   pineapple juice
¼ cup orange juice

¼ cup tomato juice
Juice of ¼ lemon
1 tsp. cornstarch
1 tbsp. water
⅓ cup diced fresh or canned
   pineapple

Cut chicken breast into 1-inch pieces and dredge in flour. Heat oil
in a wok or heavy skillet. When oil is hot, quickly stir-fry chicken
until cooked (about 3 minutes), remove, and drain on paper towels.
Combine all the juices and bring to a boil in wok. Dissolve cornstarch in water, stir into juices, return to a boil, and cook 1 minute
until mixture is thick and clear. Add chicken and pineapple, stir
well, and serve immediately.

   Purée or cut up well for infants.

1 adult and 1 child serving

/ / /

Roast Chicken in Tomato Sauce

1 roasting chicken, washed (or chicken parts)
2 cups tomato sauce (see page 283)

Preheat oven to 375°, place chicken in roasting pan breast side
down, and cook for 1 hour. Remove chicken from pan. Drain off
excess fat, add tomato sauce to pan, and stir, scraping brown glaze
from bottom of pan. Turn chicken breast side up; replace in pan,

continue cooking for another 30 minutes, and baste with sauce. Serve with the tomato sauce over rice.

Serves 4

/ / /

Baked Chicken with Tarragon

1 roasting chicken
1 cup dry white wine
1 tsp. tarragon
Dash white pepper

Wash and dry chicken and place in an ovenproof dish. Pour wine over chicken, rub with tarragon and pepper, and bake in preheated 350° oven for 1½ hours, or until juices run clear. For a crisper skin and the best flavor, baste with wine-meat juices occasionally. (The alcohol in the wine evaporates during cooking.)

Serves 4 to 5

/ / /

Groundnut Chicken Stew

4 tbsp. vegetable oil
1 medium-size onion, peeled
* and chopped*
1 stewing chicken, washed and
* cut into serving pieces*
4 medium-size tomatoes, peeled
* and chopped*

2 cups chicken stock (see page
* 281)*
½ tsp. thyme
½ cup peanut butter
6-oz. can tomato paste
3 hard-boiled eggs
2 tbsp. chopped parsley

In a large heavy pot heat oil and lightly sauté onion in it. Add chicken and brown on both sides. Add tomatoes, stock, and thyme, mix well, and bring to a boil. Reduce heat and simmer, covered, for 15 minutes. Remove enough liquid from pot to mix with peanut butter and tomato paste to make a gravy, combine well, return to pot, and simmer chicken for 45 minutes more. Serve stew over boiled rice, garnished with sliced hard-boiled eggs and parsley.

Serves 4 to 5

/ / /

Cornish Game Hens with Grapes and Orange Butter

2 Cornish game hens, washed
2 tbsp. butter, softened
1 tbsp. finely grated orange
   peel

1 tsp. minced fresh ginger
1 tsp. minced shallot
2 tbsp. melted butter
1 tbsp. soy sauce

FOR GRAPE STUFFING:

2 tbsp. butter
½ onion, peeled and chopped
2 slices day-old bread, crusts
   trimmed off and cubed

2 tbsp. minced fresh parsley
½ tsp. thyme
½ cup seedless grapes, washed

Make a pocket in each breast of the hens, using fingers to loosen skin carefully. Combine 2 tablespoons butter, orange peel, ginger, and shallot in a small bowl, and mix until smooth. Divide mixture and stuff into pockets, spreading evenly by pushing down on skin with fingers.

For stuffing melt 2 tablespoons butter in a saucepan over low heat, add onion, and sauté until golden. Add bread, parsley, and thyme and mix well. Gently stir in grapes. Fill cavities of hens about two thirds full of stuffing and truss securely.

Combine melted butter and soy sauce and, with a pastry brush, coat all sides of the game hens. Arrange hens on sides on a rack in a roasting pan. Cook in preheated 425° oven for 10 minutes. Turn to other sides and continue cooking for another 10 minutes. Reduce heat to 375°, turn hens breast side up, and continue roasting for another 40 minutes.

Serves 4

MEATS

Ground Veal Patties

1 cup, firmly packed, ground
  veal
1 clove garlic, crushed
Juice and grated rind of ¼
  lemon

1 egg, beaten
3 tbsp. corn oil
½ cup beef or chicken broth

Mix together the veal, garlic, lemon juice and rind, and egg. Form mixture into 4 balls. Refrigerate for 1 hour, then roll out each ball to ½-inch thickness. Heat oil in a skillet and fry patties for 2 minutes on each side over medium heat. Add broth and simmer gently for 10 minutes.

Makes 4 small patties

/ / /

Veal Scaloppine

Olive oil for sautéing
4 veal chops
28-oz. can plum tomatoes
1 onion, peeled and chopped
12 mushrooms, washed and
    sliced

1 bell pepper, seeded and sliced
    thin
1 tsp. oregano
Pinch red pepper

In a frying pan heat a little oil and brown chops on both sides. Break up tomatoes, add to veal, and simmer for 5 minutes. In another frying pan, sauté onion and mushrooms until tender and remove from pan. Add sliced pepper to pan and sauté until pepper is soft. Add cooked pepper to onion and mushrooms. Take ½ cup tomato mixture from the first pan and mix with the juices in the second pan. Return all ingredients to the first pan, add oregano and pinch of red pepper, stir well, and simmer for 10 minutes, or until veal is cooked through and tender.

Remove meat from bones and purée or shred for infants, and mash vegetables.

Serves 4

/ / /

Baked Ham in Vegetable Juice

A 1-lb. can ham
6-oz. can V-8 or similar vegetable juice

Place ham in a small ovenproof dish and pour vegetable juice over it. Bake in preheated 350° oven for 30 minutes, or until thoroughly heated.

Serves 4

/ / /

Scalloped Potatoes with Ham

1 cup sliced potatoes
2 slices ham, cut into 1-inch pieces
¾ cup milk
2 tbsp. butter

Grease an ovenproof dish and preheat oven to 350°. Layer potatoes
and ham in dish, bring milk to a boil and add butter, and pour over
potatoes and ham. Cover dish and bake for 1 hour, or until potatoes
are tender.

Serves 2 to 3

/ / /

Baby Pasta with Meat Sauce

3 tbsp. stelline (small star-
   shaped macaroni)
1 tbsp. finely chopped onion
1 tsp. olive oil

3 tbsp. lean ground beef
3 tbsp. tomato sauce (see page
   283), or 1 tbsp. tomato paste
   mixed with 2 tbsp. water

Cook stelline according to directions on package. In a skillet sauté
onion in olive oil until tender, add crumbled ground beef, and cook
over low heat until redness has disappeared from meat. Add tomato
sauce, mix well with meat, and simmer for 1 or 2 minutes to develop flavor. Stir mixture into cooked stelline and serve.

1 or 2 infant servings

/ / /

Beef, Bean, and Macaroni Casserole

½ lb. lean ground beef
1 small onion, peeled and
    chopped
2 cups canned tomatoes
    (reserve liquid), chopped
1 cup cooked kidney beans (see
    page 146; reserve liquid)

½ cup uncooked elbow
    macaroni
½ tsp. basil
½ tsp. oregano
½ tsp. chili powder

In a large skillet, brown beef and onion. Drain off fat. If necessary, add water to combined tomato and bean liquid to equal 1 cup, and add to skillet with tomatoes, kidney beans, macaroni, and seasonings. Cover and simmer for approximately 20 minutes, or until macaroni is tender. Stir occasionally to prevent sticking; if necessary, add more liquid during cooking.

Serves 4

/ / /

Cabbage Rolls

1 cabbage
½ onion, peeled and chopped
1 tbsp. cooking oil
½ lb. lean ground beef
¼ cup uncooked rice

1 cup tomato sauce (see page
    283)
Sufficient meat or vegetable
    stock or broth to cover rolls

Remove any torn outer leaves from cabbage, cut out core with sharp knife, being careful to keep cabbage whole. Place cabbage, base down, in a large pot, cover with boiling water, and blanch for 5 minutes. Remove, drain, and when cool separate leaves, using 8 of the best large outer leaves for the rolls. In a skillet gently sauté onion in oil until soft, then mix in a large bowl with uncooked meat, rice, parsley, and ½ cup tomato sauce. Put 1 large tablespoon of filling into each leaf and fold, envelope style, making sure it is "sealed." Place extra cabbage leaves on the bottom of a large flame-proof pan, put cabbage rolls on top of leaves, seam side down, and cover with stock. Weight rolls down with a heavy plate, cover pan, and simmer for 1¼ hours. Serve with remainder of the tomato sauce, or make a brown sauce if desired.

Serves 4

/ / /

Halloween Stew (in a Pumpkin)

2 onions, peeled and chopped
2 cloves garlic, minced
1½ lbs. stewing beef, cubed
1 tbsp. vegetable oil
2 green peppers, diced
4 tomatoes, peeled and diced
2 white potatoes, peeled and
    diced
2 sweet potatoes, peeled and
    diced

1 cup sweet corn
1 cup diced pumpkin (optional)
½ cup diced fresh peaches
    (optional)
4 cups stock or water
Salt and pepper to taste
1 pumpkin, 15 inches in
    diameter, for serving

In a large pot fry onions, garlic, and beef in oil until meat is browned and onions are tender. Add all remaining ingredients, cover with stock, bring to a boil, reduce heat, and simmer until meat is tender (1½ to 2 hours). While stew is cooking, cut a lid-size piece from top of pumpkin, remove seeds and pulp, but leave firm flesh intact. Preheat oven to 375° and steam pumpkin, with lid alongside, in ovenproof dish with 2 inches of water until tender but still firm (about 1 hour). Set pumpkin in a serving dish, carefully fill with hot stew, and replace the lid. To serve, spoon out stew and carefully cut out inside of pumpkin flesh to serve with stew if desired.

Serves 4 adults and 4 children

/ / /

Meatballs

5 oz. ground sirloin
3 tbsp. bread crumbs
2 tbsp. grated onion

4 tbsp. water
Dash salt (optional)
1 tbsp. vegetable oil

In a mixing bowl put meat, bread crumbs, onion, and water (plus salt, if desired), and mix well. Shape into small 1-inch meatballs, and fry in a little oil over low heat until cooked through.

1 adult and 1 child serving

/ / /

Meat Cakes

1 lb. lean or extra-lean ground beef
1 egg
1 tbsp. bread crumbs
A little milk, if necessary

Mix all ingredients thoroughly, using milk if necessary to hold mixture together. For each meat cake take 1 tablespoonful of meat and pat into a 2-inch round. Cook in a skillet over medium heat until meat is cooked through and all redness is gone.

Makes 12 meat cakes (May be frozen and reheated later.)

/ / /

Shepherd's Pie

1 lb. lean guard beef or lamb
1 medium onion, peeled and
 chopped
1 cup stewed tomatoes, or 2 or
 3 fresh tomatoes, peeled and
 chopped

1 tbsp. finely chopped parsley
Dash Worcestershire sauce
¼ tsp. ground pepper
4 cups hot mashed potatoes
1 tbsp. butter

Slowly brown ground meat and onion until meat is cooked and crumbly and onion is tender (add oil only if fat from meat is insufficient). Stir in tomatoes, parsley, Worcestershire sauce, and pepper; mix and heat thoroughly. Transfer mixture to a heatproof dish, top with hot mashed potatoes, and dot with butter. Put under preheated broiler and cook for 8 to 10 minutes, or until potato is golden and crisp.

Serves 4

/ / /

Zucchini Beef Skillet

1 lb. lean ground beef
1 small onion, peeled and
 chopped
1 lb. zucchini, washed and
 sliced

1 clove garlic, minced
16-oz. can whole tomatoes
Dash pepper
2 tsp. oregano

In large skillet brown ground beef with onion. Drain off fat. Add all remaining ingredients and stir. Cover and simmer for 15 minutes.

Serves 4

/ / /

Arabian Stew

2 tbsp. olive oil
1 medium-size onion, peeled
  and chopped
1 lb. stewing lamb cut into
  1-inch cubes
1 cup peeled and chopped
  tomatoes

1 tbsp. chopped fresh mint
  leaves
¼ tsp. pepper
¼ tsp. salt
8 cups hot water
1 cup cooked vermicelli

Heat oil in a large saucepan and fry onion until golden brown, add meat and brown on all sides. Add tomatoes, mint, and seasonings, stir well, and cover with hot water. Bring to a boil and simmer for 3½ hours, uncovered. Add cooked vermicelli, heat through, and serve immediately.

Purée or shred meat for infants.

Serves 4

/ / /

Greek Lamb Stew

2 lbs. stewing lamb, cut into
  1-inch cubes
3 tbsp. flour, 1 tsp. salt, and
  ½ tsp. pepper, mixed in a
  bag
2 tbsp. peanut oil
1 medium onion, peeled and
  chopped

2 cups canned tomatoes,
  strained
1 carrot, scrubbed and sliced
1 stalk celery, sliced
1 bay leaf
2 tbsp. chopped parsley
1 tsp. chopped fresh mint leaves

Dredge meat in flour and brown in oil in a large skillet. Add onion and sauté until soft, then add tomatoes, vegetables, and herbs. Cook, covered, for 1 hour over low heat, stirring occasionally. Add stock or water if more liquid is needed. Serve with a fresh vegetable, such as peas, zucchini, eggplant, okra, or potatoes, and/or pasta and bread with feta cheese and olives.

Purée or mash meat and vegetables for infants.

Serves 8

/ / /

Roast Lamb and Potatoes

1 leg of lamb
Pepper and rosemary
2 cloves garlic, sliced
6 medium-size potatoes, peeled
  and halved lengthwise

Flour
Vegetable stock (see page 282)
  or water

Rub lamb with pepper and rosemary, make small slits diagonally in skin, and insert garlic slices. Place lamb in a roasting pan and cook in preheated 325° oven for 25 to 30 minutes per pound. Baste occasionally with juices, and add potatoes around the meat approximately 1½ hours before lamb is done. Turn potatoes after 45 minutes to finish browning.

To make pan gravy, remove lamb and place on a hot platter. Remove excess fat from roasting pan, leaving 1 or 2 tablespoons. Take pan off heat, add 1 tablespoon flour to drippings, mix with a wooden spoon, scraping pan well. Return pan to low to medium heat, add vegetable stock or water, and bring to a boil. Reduce heat and simmer, stirring to prevent burning, until gravy is well blended and thickened.

Purée or finely chop meat for infants and toddlers.

Serves 6 to 8

/ / /

Leftover Lamb with Beans

Lean cooked lamb and lamb
  shank
8 cups vegetable stock (see
  page 282) or water

1 onion, peeled and quartered
1 cup small white dried beans
1 bay leaf
Leftover vegetables

Cut meat from leftover leg of lamb, trim off fat, and put meat and bone in a large heavy pan. Cover with stock or water, add onion, beans, and bay leaf, and bring to a boil over medium heat. Reduce heat and simmer for 2 hours. Remove bone from pan. Add leftover vegetables (especially potatoes, carrots, and peas) and reheat.

For adults, ½ cup of red wine and other seasonings may be added to stew, if desired.

Serves 4

/ / /

Norwegian Lamb and Cabbage

2 lbs. lean lamb, cut into
  1-inch cubes
2 heads cabbage, washed and
  sliced
½ tsp. salt

2 tbsp. flour
Handful whole peppercorns,
  tied in cheesecloth
½ cup water

Layer lamb and cabbage in a heavy pan, starting with a layer of meat. Sprinkle a little salt and flour between each layer. Add water and peppercorns, cover pan, and simmer on top of stove for 2 to 3 hours, occasionally stirring (carefully) to prevent burning and to mix in peppercorn flavor. Serve with boiled potatoes.

For infants purée or finely chop meat and cabbage.

Serves 6 to 8

/ / /

Puréed Kidneys with Carrots

½ lb. lamb kidneys, halved and cleaned, fat removed
2 medium-size carrots, scrubbed and sliced
⅓ cup milk or homemade vegetable or chicken stock (see page 282 or
*   page 281)*

Soak kidneys in cold water for 1 hour, then put in a saucepan with water sufficient to cover. Bring to a boil, reduce heat to medium, and cook for 1 hour, adding carrots for the last 20 minutes. Drain kidneys and carrots, put in a food processor, fitted with a steel blade, or in a blender, add milk or stock, and purée until smooth.

3 or 4 child servings (May be frozen and reheated later.)

/ / /

Baked Liver with Cider

1 lb. calf's liver, sliced
1 tbsp. whole wheat flour
½ tsp. salt
⅛ tsp. pepper
2 tbsp. peanut oil

½ onion, peeled and chopped
1 stalk celery, tops included,
*   washed and chopped*
1 carrot, scrubbed and sliced
1 cup hot sweet apple cider

Dredge liver in flour mixed with salt and pepper. Put oil in an ovenproof dish, add chopped onion, then slices of liver, and top with celery and carrot. Pour about ⅓ cup hot cider over liver, cover, and put in preheated 325° oven. After approximately 20 minutes, add another ⅓ cup cider, and final ⅓ cup 20 minutes later, or when previous cider has nearly evaporated. (Total cooking time, 1 hour.)

Serves 4

/ / /

Broiled Liver Patties

½ lb. calf's liver
Chicken, beef, or vegetable
   broth to cover (1 to 2 cups)

½ onion, peeled and chopped
1 egg
3 tbsp. chopped parsley

Put liver, broth, and onion in a medium-size pan, cover, bring to a boil, and cook until liver is tender. Drain, reserving a little broth. In a blender or food processor, purée liver and onion with egg and parsley, adding a small amount of broth if necessary. Form mixture into 2 or 3 patties. Put under preheated broiler and brown on both sides. If this is more than desired quantity, place extra patties between layers of wax paper, wrap in foil, and store in freezer.

2 to 3 child servings

/ / /

Liver Loaf

1 lb. calf's liver
½ tbsp. finely chopped onion
½ tbsp. chopped parsley
1 cup bread crumbs

¼ cup meat broth
½ cup milk
1 tbsp. melted butter
2 eggs, beaten

Purée liver, onion, and parsley in a food processor or blender. Mix together bread crumbs, broth, milk, butter, and beaten eggs, and blend thoroughly with the liver purée. Pour mixture into a greased ovenproof dish, place dish in a pan of hot water, and bake in preheated 350° oven for 1 hour, or until loaf is cooked through and firm. Liver should lose all pinkness and be a grayish brown when cooked.

Serves 4

/ / /

Sautéed Calf's Liver

1 small piece calf's liver   Dash pepper
  (about 2 oz.)   1 tbsp. peanut or safflower oil
1 tsp. flour   2 tbsp. milk

Dry liver with a paper towel and coat in flour mixed with the pepper. Heat oil in a frying pan, add liver, and cook over medium heat, turning at least twice, until all redness is gone and liver is cooked through. Cut meat into 2 or 3 pieces and, using steel blade, place in a food processor or blender along with milk, and purée until smooth.

1 infant serving

GRAINS AND PASTA

Cooked Barley

1 tbsp. barley
2 cups water

Bring barley and water to a boil in a saucepan. Reduce heat, cover, and simmer for 1½ hours until barley is tender.

Small amounts (up to 2 ounces or so) of cooked meat and/or vegetables may be added to the barley, if desired. Heat through for a minute or two before serving.

Makes ⅓ cup (without meat or vegetables)

/ / /

Bulgur Pilaf

4 tbsp. butter
1 small onion, peeled and
   minced
1 coil vermicelli, broken into
   pieces

1 cup cracked wheat (bulgur)
2½ cups chicken stock (see
   page 281)

Melt butter in a pan, add onion and vermicelli, and brown lightly. Add cracked wheat and chicken stock, and bring to a boil. Stir well to mix, cover, reduce heat, and simmer for 20 minutes. Remove from heat and let stand for 5 minutes. Fluff with fork before serving.

Serves 4

/ / /

Cornmeal Mush

2 cups water
½ cup cornmeal

Bring 1½ cups of water to a boil over medium heat. Mix remaining water with cornmeal and add to boiling water, stirring constantly. Cook over low heat for 5 minutes, stirring continually until ready.

Serves 4

/ / /

Millet Cereal

½ cup millet, well rinsed
¼ cup powdered skim milk
1½ cups water

Combine ingredients in a heavy pan, bring to a boil, reduce heat, and simmer for 10 minutes, stirring occasionally. Remove pan from heat, cover, and let stand for 30 minutes.

Serves 4

/ / /

Millet Soufflé

½ cup millet (makes 2 cups)
2 cups water
3 egg yolks, beaten
⅔ cup milk

1 cup grated jack, cheddar, or
    Swiss cheese
3 egg whites, stiffly beaten

Mix millet with water in saucepan and bring to a boil. Reduce heat, cover, and simmer for 30 minutes.

Mix well 1¾ cups cooked millet, egg yolks, milk, and half the grated cheese, and fold in egg whites gently. Pour mixture into a well-greased soufflé dish and top with remaining cheese. Place dish in a larger pan of hot water and bake in preheated 350° oven for approximately 45 minutes, or until set. Test after 30 minutes with a knife; if soufflé is cooked, knife should be clean on removal.

Serves 4

/ / /

Basmati Rice

1 cup basmati (Indian) rice
2 cups water
1 tbsp. butter

Pick impurities out of rice and wash well under cold water, using a
fine sieve. Move rice around with hands until water runs clear.
Bring 2 cups water to a boil, add rice, and stir with a fork. Reduce
heat, cover, and cook for 10 minutes. Remove from heat and let
stand for 10 more minutes. Add 1 tablespoon butter and fluff rice
with fork before serving.

Serves 3

/ / /

Rice with Cheese

1 cup cooked rice
½ cup milk
½ cup grated Parmesan or Romano cheese

Put rice in a small saucepan and add a little milk. Over medium
heat alternately add grated cheese and remaining milk, stirring constantly. Continue to simmer for a few minutes until the flavors are
blended.

1 adult and 1 child serving

/ / /

Italian Rice and Avocado Salad

½ cup rice
1¼ cups water, in all
2 medium-size zucchini,
    washed and coarsely grated
1 lb. sweet Italian sausages
1 tbsp. vegetable oil

2 avocados, peeled, pitted, and
    sliced
1 large tomato, peeled and
    chopped
¾ cup chopped parsley
Italian Dressing (see below)

Cook ½ cup rice in 1 cup water in a medium-size pan. When done, stir in zucchini, cover, and set aside. Pierce sausages with a fork and place in a skillet with ¼ cup water, cover, and simmer for 10 minutes. Drain off liquid. Add oil to skillet and cook sausages over medium-low heat, tossing occasionally, for 8 minutes, or until cooked through and browned. Drain sausages, then halve and cut into strips lengthwise. Combine with rice-zucchini mixture, add avocados, tomato, and parsley, and toss with Italian dressing.

ITALIAN DRESSING:

¼ cup vinegar
2 tsp. oregano
1 tsp. rosemary
¼ tsp. salt

⅛ tsp. black pepper
1 medium-size clove garlic,
    crushed
¼ cup olive oil

Combine all ingredients except olive oil in a blender or food processor and blend well. With machine at low speed, gradually add olive oil and continue blending until thoroughly mixed. Makes ⅔ cup of dressing.

Serves 4

/ / /

Rice Royal

1 cup uncooked rice
1½ cups grated cheddar cheese
2 tbsp. butter
1 cup finely chopped parsley

Cook rice. Add butter, grated cheese, and parsley while rice is still hot. Stir to mix well and serve immediately.

Serves 4

/ / /

Tabbouleh Salad

¼ cup finely cracked wheat
  (bulgur)
½ cup minced parsley
1 cup peeled, seeded, and
  chopped tomatoes
¼ cup chopped fresh mint

¼ cup lemon juice
2 tbsp. green onion, finely
  chopped
¼ cup olive oil
Romaine lettuce

Soak cracked wheat for 10 minutes in enough water to cover. Drain and squeeze as dry as possible in a clean white towel. Place cracked wheat in a large bowl. Add all ingredients except oil and lettuce and mix well. Let stand for 30 minutes to allow flavors to blend, then add oil, mixing and tossing lightly. Serve on a bed of romaine lettuce.

Serves 4 to 6

/ / /

Beans and Broccoli with Stars

2 tbsp. stelline (cooked according to directions on package)
2 tbsp. small dried white beans, cooked (see page 146)
½ cup tomato sauce (see page 283)
1 small floweret broccoli, steamed and diced

Combine stelline (star-shaped pasta) with beans and tomato sauce
in a small pan. Mix and cook over low heat for 5 minutes, then add
broccoli to heat through (1 minute).

1 child serving

/ / /

Cottage Cheese and Noodle Casserole

8 oz. broad egg noodles
1 egg, lightly beaten
2 cups small-curd cottage
  cheese

¼ cup melted butter
¼ cup bread crumbs

Cook noodles according to directions on package and drain. Mix
lightly beaten egg into cottage cheese. Grease an ovenproof dish,
place in it a layer of noodles followed by the cottage cheese, and
top with remaining noodles. Mix butter and bread crumbs together
and cover noodles with mixture. Bake in preheated 375° oven for
30 minutes.

Serves 2 to 3

/ / /

Fettuccine

8 oz. fettuccine
1 tsp. vegetable oil
1 cup cream (or half-and-half)
1 egg yolk

2 oz. unsalted butter
Freshly ground pepper
½ cup freshly grated Parmesan
  cheese

Cook noodles in a large pan of boiling water with vegetable oil until tender but firm (al dente). Warm an ovenproof casserole. Beat cream and egg yolk together well, and gently heat butter in a small saucepan. When noodles are cooked, drain thoroughly, place them in warmed casserole, pour butter and cream-egg mixture over them, add pepper, and mix gently. Gradually add Parmesan cheese, about 1 tablespoon at a time, until blended, reserving 2 tablespoonsful for garnish, and continue to toss. Sprinkle remaining cheese over fettuccine and serve immediately.

Serves 2 to 3

/ / /

Macaroni Broccoli Sauté

2 cups cooked broccoli
4 tbsp. olive oil
1 clove garlic, peeled and
  crushed

¼ cup diced pimiento
1 cup small cooked macaroni

Finely chop broccoli. In a skillet heat oil and add garlic and pimiento. Mix and cook for 30 seconds, then add cooked macaroni and broccoli. Cook over low heat until flavors are well blended and ingredients are heated through.

1 adult and 1 child serving

/ / /

Macaroni Marinara

⅓ cup cooked tubettini (or other small pasta)
¼ cup marinara sauce (see page 283)
1 small cooked potato, diced

Mix ingredients together in a small pan and simmer for 2 to 3 minutes.

1 or 2 child servings

/ / /

Macaroni Salad

1 cup small macaroni
1 cup peeled and thinly sliced
  cucumber
1 cup diced tomatoes
½ cup chopped celery
¼ cup chopped green pepper
6½-oz. can tuna, shredded
  (optional)

1 tsp. dill
½ cup mayonnaise
¼ cup ready-made Italian
  dressing
Lettuce for garnish
1 hard-boiled egg, sliced

Cook, drain, and chill macaroni. Mix together all ingredients except egg until blended. Arrange washed lettuce leaves in a salad bowl, covering base and sides. Add macaroni salad (plus shredded tuna if desired) and decorate with hard-boiled egg slices. Chill until ready to serve.

Serves 4

/ / /

Baked Mostaccioli

½ onion, peeled and chopped
1 clove garlic, minced
1 tbsp. olive oil
4 oz. ground beef
1 tbsp. chopped parsley

2 cups tomato sauce (see page
  283)
8 oz. mostaccioli *pasta, cooked*
1 cup cheddar cheese, thinly
  sliced or grated

In a skillet cook onion and garlic in oil until tender and drain. In same skillet brown beef with parsley until crumbly, and drain off any excess fat. Add tomato sauce, bring to a boil, reduce heat, and simmer for 15 minutes, stirring occasionally. Meanwhile, cook pasta until tender, drain well, and place in a heatproof casserole. When meat sauce is ready, pour over pasta and mix well. Cover completely with sliced or grated cheese and pop under preheated broiler until cheese is melted and bubbling.

Serves 2 to 3

/ / /

Pasta and Chick Peas

1 cup cooked ditalini
1 cup cooked chick peas
  (garbanzo beans)
2 cups canned peeled Italian
  tomatoes, crushed

3 tbsp. olive oil
1 tbsp. chopped parsley
¼ tsp. basil
1 clove garlic, whole
⅛ tsp. pepper

Combine all ingredients except chick peas and ditalini in a saucepan, bring to a boil, and simmer for 20 minutes. Remove garlic clove, add chick peas and ditalini, and simmer for 1 or 2 minutes, stirring until well blended and heated through.

Serves 2 to 3

/ / /

Pasta e Fagioli
(Macaroni and Beans)

1 tsp. olive oil
Small clove garlic, peeled
⅓ cup canned Italian plum
   tomatoes, chopped
¼ tsp. oregano

Pinch pepper
4 tbsp. cooked ditalini or small
   elbow macaroni
2 tbsp. small dried white
   beans, cooked (see page 146)

Heat oil in a pan and cook garlic clove for 1 minute. Add tomatoes, oregano, and pepper, and simmer for 5 minutes. Remove garlic. Add pasta and beans to the sauce and simmer for 5 more minutes, stirring occasionally to blend.

1 child serving

/ / /

Pasta with Peas

¼ onion, finely chopped
2 tbsp. olive oil
½ cup canned Italian
   tomatoes, sieved or puréed

Pinch each oregano and pepper
½ cup cooked tubettini (or
   other small pasta)
1 cup fresh or frozen small peas

Sauté onion in oil in a medium-size pan until tender. Add tomatoes and seasoning, bring to a boil, reduce heat, and simmer for 5 minutes. Add tubettini and peas, stir gently, and continue to simmer for another 5 minutes.

1 adult and 1 child serving

/ / /

Stelline with Cottage Cheese

3 tbsp. stelline (or other small pasta)
1 tbsp. butter, melted
4 tbsp. small-curd cottage cheese

Cook pasta according to directions on package, drain, and add melted butter. Add cottage cheese and toss well.

1 child serving

SOUPS

Cream of Broccoli Soup

2 lbs. cooked and cooled broccoli (stems are good for soup)
2 cups vegetable or chicken stock (see page 282 or page 281)

2 cups milk
4 tbsp. butter
½ tsp. garlic powder
¼ tsp. white pepper

Put broccoli in a food processor or blender with some of the stock. Purée, pour mixture into a saucepan, and add all other ingredients. Heat over a very low flame, stirring well until heated through.

Serves 4 to 6

/ / /

Celery Soup

1 bunch celery, tops included,
   washed
4 leeks, white parts only, well
   washed
3 potatoes, peeled

5 mushrooms, washed
1½ quarts water
¼ cup tamari or soy sauce
1 tsp. celery salt
⅛ tsp. each thyme and basil

Slice vegetables thin. Place all vegetables except mushrooms in a pot with 1½ quarts of water and bring to a boil. Add seasonings, cover, reduce heat, and simmer for 10 minutes. In a blender or food processor, purée ingredients in batches. Return purée to the pot, add sliced mushrooms, and simmer for 30 minutes. Stir frequently and make sure the soup does not scorch.

Serves 6

/ / /

Cold Cream of Avocado Soup

3 ripe avocados, peeled, pitted,
   and diced
1 cup chicken stock (see page
   281)
2 tsp. lime or lemon juice

1 clove garlic, peeled and
   minced
½ tsp. salt
1 cup half-and-half (or
   whipping cream)

Combine avocados and chicken stock in a blender or food processor, and purée until smooth. Add lime or lemon juice, garlic, and salt, and continue to blend. Pour into a bowl and stir in half-and-half or cream. Chill well before serving.

Serves 2

/ / /

Cream of Tomato Soup

2 tbsp. butter
½ onion, peeled and chopped
1 medium-size potato, peeled
  and cubed
1½ cups chicken stock (see
  page 281)

5 ripe tomatoes, peeled and
  chopped
1½ cups milk
2 hard-boiled eggs, halved
  (optional)
½ cup cooked tiny macaroni
  (optional)

Melt butter in a heavy pot and sauté onion and potato in it for 3 minutes, or until onion is glazed. Add chicken stock to pot, bring to a boil, reduce heat, and simmer until potato is tender (between 5 and 10 minutes). Place tomatoes in a food processor or blender, add broth and potato, and purée until smooth. Return soup to pot, add milk, and heat thoroughly but *do not allow to boil*. Stir in macaroni, if desired, and keep over low heat until warmed. Put egg halves in bowl and ladle soup over.

Small pieces of steamed broccoli, cauliflower, or squash may also be added for variety.

Serves 4

/ / /

Karin's Health Soup

1 cup soybeans, soaked
  overnight
4 cups vegetable or chicken
  stock (see page 282 or page
  281), or water

3 potatoes, peeled and diced
½ cabbage, diced
2 cups chopped broccoli

Bring soybeans to a boil in stock or water, reduce heat, and simmer for 2 hours in a covered kettle. (If necessary, add more liquid.) Add potatoes, cabbage, and broccoli, and cook for another 15 minutes. Purée soup in a food processor, or mash the beans and vegetables, before serving.

Serves 6

/ / /

Lentil Soup

1 cup lentils, washed
4 cups water
4 tbsp. butter or safflower oil
1 large potato, peeled and
  diced

3 stalk celery, sliced thin
2 carrots, scrubbed and sliced
  thin

Cook lentils (see page 148) in water until almost tender, about 30 minutes. Heat butter or oil in a frying pan and in it gently sauté potato, celery, and carrots. (These vegetables can be added to lentils without sautéing first, if desired. Sautéing adds flavor.) Combine all vegetables with lentils, bring to a boil, reduce heat, and simmer for 10 minutes, or until vegetables are soft. For older children and adults, thyme, salt, and a vegetable, chicken, or beef bouillon cube may be added before simmering.

   For infants and toddlers, purée or mash mixture to desired consistency.

Serves 4

/ / /

Split Pea Soup

1 onion, peeled and chopped
2 tbsp. olive oil
1 cup dried split peas, soaked
   overnight
4 cups water
½ tsp. thyme

1 bay leaf
1 large carrot, scrubbed and
   sliced
1 large potato, peeled and
   diced
1 tbsp. finely chopped parsley

Sauté onion in oil until tender; set aside. In a large pot combine peas, water, thyme, and bay leaf. Bring to a boil and cook for 2 minutes. Let stand for 1 hour. Add onion, carrot, and potato, and simmer for 30 to 45 minutes. Remove bay leaf before serving and garnish with parsley.

Serves 6

/ / /

Syrian Lentil Soup

1 medium onion, peeled and
   chopped
1 tbsp. olive oil
1 cup lentils, washed
½ cup rice
6 cups lamb stock (or other
   meat stock) or water

10-oz. package frozen spinach,
   or bunch fresh spinach,
   washed and trimmed
1 tsp. salt
½ tsp. cumin
Juice of ½ lemon

Cook onion in oil in a large pot until soft. Add lentils, rice, and stock (or water), and bring to a boil. Reduce heat and simmer gently for 1 hour. Add spinach, salt, and cumin, and cook for another 15 minutes. Stir in lemon juice before serving.

Serves 6 to 8

/ / /

Vegetable Barley Soup

¼ cup barley
4 cups vegetable or chicken
  stock (see page 282 or page
  281)
¼ onion, chopped
1 clove garlic, minced
1 tbsp. butter or 2 tbsp.
  cooking oil

1 carrot, scrubbed and diced
1 small stalk celery, sliced
½ potato, scrubbed and diced
5 mushrooms, washed and
  sliced
½ tsp. thyme
2 tbsp. chopped parsley

Soak barley in cold water for 1 hour, drain, and combine in a large pot with 2 cups of the chicken stock. Bring to a boil, reduce heat, and simmer for 45 minutes, covered, until barley is soft. In a skillet sauté onion and garlic in butter or oil until tender. Add carrot, celery, potato, and mushrooms, and simmer for 10 minutes, stirring frequently. Add vegetables and thyme, plus remaining 2 cups stock, to barley. Simmer for 1 hour, stirring occasionally to prevent sticking. (Add more stock or other liquid if necessary to thin.) Add parsley just before serving.

Serves 6

/ / /

Yam Soup

1 tbsp. peanut or other
  vegetable oil
1 medium-size onion, peeled
  and chopped
2 tomatoes, peeled and chopped

½ lb. yams or sweet potatoes,
  peeled and cubed
1¼ cups vegetable or chicken
  stock (see page 282 or page
  281)
2 tbsp. chopped parsley

Heat oil in a pot and sauté onion and chopped tomatoes in it until onion is tender. Add yams and stock, and bring to a boil. Reduce heat and simmer over low heat until yams are tender (about 30 minutes). Press mixture through a sieve, or blend or process, to achieve a purée. Return soup to pot to reheat. Garnish with parsley before serving.

Serves 2

/ / /

Homemade Chicken Soup

1 cup homemade chicken stock (see page 281)
1 tbsp. finely chopped cooked chicken
½ carrot, scrubbed and shredded
2 tbsp. pastina or 3 tbsp. cooked rice

Bring stock to a boil in a saucepan, add all other ingredients, and continue to cook at a low boil for 5 minutes, or until carrot and pastina are done. Variations on this soup can be made by adding such vegetables as peas, beans, broccoli, spinach, squash (summer, banana, or acorn), or zucchini.

1 adult and 1 child serving

/ / /

Chicken and Papaya Soup

1 chicken breast, boned and
  skinned
1 tbsp. vegetable oil
¼ onion, chopped
1 small clove garlic, minced
4 cups homemade chicken stock
  (see page 281) or water
1 tomato, peeled and chopped

½ unripe peeled papaya, cut
  into finger-width pieces
1 leaf lemon grass, washed,
  rubbed and tied (4-inch strip
  of lemon peel can be
  substituted)
½ bunch fresh spinach,
  washed, stems removed
3 cups cooked rice

Cut chicken into 1-inch cubes and sauté in vegetable oil with onion and garlic for 3 minutes, or until chicken is lightly browned on all sides. Bring chicken stock or water to a boil in a large pan. Add chicken mixture and chopped tomato. Reduce heat, cover, and simmer for 45 minutes, or until chicken is tender. Add papaya and cook for 10 minutes more, adding lemon grass after 5 minutes. The spinach should be added at the last minute to preserve freshness and color. For each serving, place ½ cup cooked rice in a bowl and ladle soup over it.

Serves 6

/ / /

Chicken Soup with Speck
(Mini Dumplings)

Speck batter (see below)
1 cup chicken stock (see page 281)
1 tbsp. finely chopped cooked chicken
½ carrot, scrubbed and shredded

Make batter. Bring stock to a boil in a saucepan. Dip a fork into *speck* batter and shake batter off into boiling stock, using about half the mixture. (Save remainder to use soon in another soup.) Add grated carrot and chopped chicken to soup, and continue to cook at a low boil until carrots are tender.

SPECK BATTER:

1 egg, well beaten   *3 level tbsp. flour*

Beat flour into egg until a smooth batter is formed. It should be about the consistency of a pancake batter, not too thick and not liquid.

1 adult and 1 child serving

/ / /

Leftover Turkey Soup

Turkey carcass, stripped of all   *2 carrots, scrubbed*
  meat (reserve meat)   *2 stalks celery, halved*
1 medium-size onion, peeled   *Any leftover vegetables*
  and halved

Put turkey carcass in a large kettle and cover with water. Add onion, carrots, celery, and turkey meat. Bring to a boil, reduce heat, and simmer on very low heat for 3 hours. Remove bones from broth. Strain out vegetables through a sieve, and add leftover potatoes, peas, cauliflower, etc., to the soup. Add seasonings for adults.

Serves 6 to 8

/ / /

Cholent
(Meat, Bean, and Vegetable Soup)

2 lbs. brisket of beef, trimmed
   of fat
Chicken fat or vegetable oil
1 onion, peeled and chopped
1 clove garlic, peeled and
   minced
1 cup dried lima beans, soaked
   overnight
½ cup barley

4 medium-size potatoes, peeled
4 carrots, scrubbed
2 turnips, peeled and halved
½ tbsp. paprika
1 tsp. salt
½ tsp. pepper
¼ tsp. each cinnamon and
   ground ginger (optional)
½ cup minced parsley

In a large Dutch oven, brown meat in chicken fat or oil together with chopped onion and garlic. Drain lima beans and add to meat, and add all other ingredients except parsley. Add enough boiling water to cover and bake in preheated 350° oven for 4 hours. To serve, break off pieces of meat from the brisket, cover with the soup, and garnish with parsley. Serve with challah bread (see page 249).

For infants and toddlers, purée or chop meat (and vegetables) to desired consistency.

Serves 8

/ / /

Pot-au-Feu

Plan to make this for a party or holiday:

5 lbs. beef bones

5 carrots, scrubbed

2 onions, peeled and quartered

2 leeks, white parts only,
    carefully washed

3 stalks celery, with tops,
    washed

1 tbsp. salt

Bouquet garni *(2 bay leaves, 4
    sprigs parsley, 1 tbsp. thyme,
    1 tbsp. peppercorns; tie in
    cheesecloth tightly and drop
    into pot)*

¾ lb. lean beef, cubed

1 whole chicken, cut up

1 lb. Polish or veal sausage

12 potatoes, peeled and halved

1 lb. carrots, scrubbed and cut
    into thirds

1 tsp. ground pepper

Bunch finely chopped parsley

The day before: Cook beef bones, the 5 carrots, onions, leeks, and celery in large pot of water with salt and the *bouquet garni* for 4 to 5 hours. Keep covered and constantly simmering. Let cool, then pour broth through colander lined with double layer of cheesecloth into another large pot. Discard all bones and vegetables. Refrigerate overnight.

The next day: Remove hard fat from broth, which will be like a gelatin, and return to heat, bringing slowly to a full boil. Add beef and chicken pieces and simmer for 1 hour. Finally, add sausage, potatoes, remaining pound of carrots, and ground pepper, and boil for 20 minutes, or until sausages and vegetables are cooked. Serve pot-au-feu sprinkled with plenty of chopped parsley. Accompany with crusty French bread.

This soup is perfect for all age groups. For under-two-year-olds, just purée or cut up finely some meat and vegetables. If desired, thyme, salt, or other seasonings may be added for adults.

Serves 12 or 16

/ / /

Bean, Rice, and Vegetable Soup

1 onion, peeled and chopped
2 tbsp. olive oil
1 quart lamb or other meat
   stock
⅓ cup dried kidney beans,
   cooked (see page 146)
½ cup cooked or canned
   garbanzo beans (chick peas)

½ cup lentils
⅓ cup raw long-grained rice
1 medium beet, cooked and cut
   into thin strips
1 cup cooked spinach, chopped
¼ cup lemon juice
Plain yogurt (optional)

Gently sauté onion in olive oil. In a large pot combine onion, stock, kidney beans, garbanzo beans, lentils, and rice. Bring to a boil, cover, and simmer for 1 hour. Add beet, spinach, and lemon juice, and continue to simmer for 4 minutes before serving to blend flavors. Top with yogurt, if desired.

Serves 6

/ / /

Black Bean Soup

½ cup dried black beans,
   soaked overnight
4 cups water
1 bay leaf

2 tbsp. oil
3 cloves garlic, peeled and
   sliced
1 onion, peeled and chopped

1 green or red sweet pepper,
   diced
½ tsp. cumin

1 tbsp. soy sauce
1 tbsp. chopped parsley

Boil beans in water with bay leaf, reduce heat, and simmer for 20 minutes. Meanwhile, bring oil to medium heat in a skillet. Add garlic and onion and sauté until tender. Add pepper and cumin and sauté for 2 to 3 minutes more. Remove from pan, drain, add to beans when they have cooked 20 minutes, and simmer for another 20 minutes. Add soy sauce in the last minute or two of cooking, and garnish with parsley.

Serves 4

/ / /

White Bean and Cabbage Soup

4 oz. small dried white beans,
   soaked overnight
5 cups boiling water
1 bay leaf
8 oz. cooked ham, cubed
⅛ tsp. black pepper
¼ tsp. thyme

8 oz. cabbage, washed and
   shredded
½ onion, peeled and chopped
1 carrot, scrubbed and thinly
   sliced
1 turnip, peeled and chopped
¼ cup minced parsley
½ tsp. salt

Rinse beans well and place in a large pan. Cover with 5 cups boiling water, bring back to a boil, and cook for 2 minutes. Cover and let stand for 1 hour while preparing vegetables. Return beans to a boil, add bay leaf, ham, black pepper, and thyme, partially cover, and simmer for 1 hour until beans are tender. Remove bay leaf and add cabbage, onion, carrot, and turnip, and simmer for 1 more hour, still partially covered. Stir in parsley and salt before serving.

Serves 4

/ / /

Yellow Pea Soup with Vegetables and Sausage

1 cup dried yellow peas, soaked
   overnight
4 cups vegetable or chicken
   stock (see page 282 or page
   281) or water
3 potatoes, peeled and diced

3 carrots, scrubbed and
   chopped
½ tsp. thyme
1 mild cooked sausage,
   chopped into 1-inch pieces
   (optional)

Bring peas to boil in stock or water, and cook until almost tender. Add all other ingredients, return to a boil, reduce heat, and simmer for 20 more minutes. Finely mash peas, potatoes and carrots, and chop optional sausage before serving to infants.

Serves 6

/ / /

Soup Dumplings

1 tbsp. butter
1 egg, beaten
3½ tbsp. all-purpose flour

Beat butter until soft, add egg, and mix well. Sift in flour and continue to mix until smooth batter is formed. Drop ¼ teaspoon of batter at a time into simmering soup or stew, and cook for 5 minutes.

BREADS

Challah
(Braided Egg Bread)

*1 yeast cake or envelope dry
   yeast*
½ cup lukewarm water
¼ lb. (1 stick) unsalted butter
½ cup warm milk
2 tsp. sugar
6 eggs, beaten

*2 cups unbleached all-purpose
   flour*
*2 cups hard-wheat white-bread
   flour*
½ tsp. salt
1 egg, beaten with 1 tsp. water
2 tbsp. sesame or poppy seeds

Lightly grease a large bowl and baking sheet and set aside. Dissolve
yeast in lukewarm water in a large glass or plastic mixing bowl.
Melt butter, add to warm milk, then add sugar and stir over low
heat until sugar is dissolved. When temperature is approximately
100° add milk mixture to yeast, then add beaten eggs. Sift in flours
and salt, and mix well until dough is formed. Turn out onto a lightly
floured board and knead until smooth and elastic (about 10 minutes). Place dough in the greased bowl, turning to coat all sides,
and cover with a clean cloth. Set in a warm place and allow to rise
until double in volume, about 2 hours. Punch down dough, knead
briefly, and set aside for 10 minutes. Place dough on lightly floured
board and cut in half. Make 3 pieces out of each half and roll each
piece into a 12-inch-long rope. Lay 3 ropes beside each other and
braid together loosely. Pinch both ends together to secure. Place
loaf on a greased baking sheet. Repeat process with second half of
the dough. Brush tops with beaten egg and sprinkle with poppy

seeds. Cover with a clean cloth and allow to again double in volume.

Bake loaves in preheated 350° oven for about 45 minutes, or until golden brown. Bread should sound hollow when tapped. Remove from baking sheet and cool on racks.

Makes 2 loaves

/ / /

Chapatis
(Indian Bread)

1 cup whole wheat flour	2 tbsp. ghee (clarified butter;
1 cup all-purpose flour	following recipe)
1 tsp. salt	¾ cup hot (not boiling) water
	from faucet

Put dry ingredients into a deep bowl, add ghee, and mix well with fingers. Add water with one hand while continuing to mix with the other. When dough becomes pliable and forms a smooth ball, stop adding water. Knead dough until it is very elastic. With pastry brush, cover dough with a thin film of ghee, and let stand while preparing to roll it out. Lightly flour a pastry board or other surface, then with hands, roll dough into a tube about 1½ inches in diameter. Cut pieces about the size of large eggs and form into round balls. Roll out with a rolling pin until each piece is approximately 6 inches in diameter and very thin. Preheat a griddle or skillet and cook chapatis for about 30 seconds on each side. Then, using tongs, hold each chapati over open flame until it puffs up. Remove immediately and brush with ghee. Pile chapatis one on top of another under a clean cloth until all are cooked. Serve immediately.

Makes 8 chapatis

/ / /

Ghee
(Clarified Butter)

Ghee is butter that has all its milk solids removed. It is used in many recipes from India and neighboring countries.

Melt 1 pound of butter in a heavy 1-quart saucepan over medium-low heat. The butter should bubble and foam, but do not let it burn. Skim off foam from top and discard. Continue to heat butter over low heat until it foams again. Skim off foam again, and repeat until all foam disappears and the butter is a clear yellow liquid. Remove from heat and let cool for 5 minutes. Strain into a glass container through cheesecloth or a fine sieve; stop when white sediment in the liquid comes to the surface.

If the ghee is absolutely pure, it can be stored for long periods of time without refrigeration. It will become solid if stored in the refrigerator, but can be liquified by heating over a low flame.

/ / /

Corn Bread

1 egg
1 cup milk
1¼ cups unbleached white
   flour
¾ cup whole-grain cornmeal

4 tbsp. sugar
5 tsp. baking powder
¼ tsp. salt
2 tbsp. melted butter

Beat egg and mix with milk. Sift in all dry ingredients, add melted butter, and beat together until smooth. Butter a 9-inch pie dish and pour in batter. Bake in preheated 375° oven for 30 minutes, or until bread is light brown around the edges.

Serves 6

/ / /

Marion Cunningham's Health Bread*

2 cups warm water, in all
2 envelopes active dry yeast
4 tbsp. instant grain beverage
 (Postum)
⅓ cup dark molasses
⅓ cup cracked wheat

⅓ cup instant nonfat dry milk,
 or 1 cup whole milk
2 tsp. salt
½ cup toasted sunflower seeds
1 cup whole wheat flour
1 cup rye flour
3 to 4 cups all-purpose flour

Sprinkle yeast over ½ cup of warm water (115°) in a small bowl, stir, and let dissolve for 5 minutes. In a large bowl combine remaining 2 cups water and all other ingredients but *only 1 cup* of the all-purpose flour. Add yeast liquid and beat vigorously for 1 full minute, then add enough all-purpose flour to make a manageable dough. Turn dough out onto a lightly floured board, knead for 2 minutes, then let rise for 10 minutes. Add enough of remaining flour to dough so that it is not sticky, and continue kneading until it is smooth and elastic. Put dough in a large greased bowl, cover, and let rise until double in bulk in a warm draft-free area. Turn dough out, punch down, and cut in half. Form each piece into a loaf and place in greased loaf pans. Cover pans lightly with clean towel and put in a warm spot to rise until dough reaches tops of pans. Make two diagonal slashes across the top of each loaf with a sharp knife. Bake in preheated 375° oven for 50 minutes. Remove loaves from pans and let cool on racks.

Makes 2 loaves

---

*From *The Fannie Farmer Cookbook*, Twelfth Edition, by Fannie Farmer, revised by Marion Cunningham with Jeri Laber. Copyright © 1979 by Fannie Farmer Cookbook Corporation. Reprinted by permission of Alfred A. Knopf, Inc.

/ / /

Mexican Flour Tortillas

4 cups all-purpose flour
2 tsp. salt
½ cup shortening
1 cup lukewarm water

Sift flour and salt into a large mixing bowl. Add shortening and with fingers mix until well blended. Add lukewarm water and mix well. Turn dough out onto a lightly floured board and knead 50 times. Divide dough into 12 equal pieces and form each piece into a ball. Cover with a clean cloth and let stand for 15 minutes. Roll out each ball into a round tortilla 8 inches in diameter. Cook on a moderately hot griddle, or in an ungreased skillet, until golden brown in spots, turning once without breaking the air bubbles.

Makes 12 tortillas

/ / /

Norwegian Potato Bread

6 medium potatoes, peeled and cut up
¼ cup milk
¼ cup butter
2½ to 3 cups all-purpose flour

Boil potatoes until very soft. Drain (save water for soups or stock). Mash potatoes thoroughly and whip in milk and butter until light and fluffy. Cool in refrigerator. When chilled, add half the flour and beat until smooth. Beat in enough remaining flour to make a soft dough. Cut off pieces big enough to roll out into rounds ⅛ inch thick and 6 inches wide. Heat ungreased griddle until water drops bounce when dropped on it. Place potato-bread rounds on griddle and cook until brown spots appear. Turn and keep turning until bread is dry and lightly covered with brown spots. Cool and serve with butter and goat cheese.

The same recipe can be achieved with 1 cup leftover mashed potatoes, ½ cup all-purpose flour, and ¼ cup milk. Mix all ingredients into a smooth dough, adding extra flour if necessary to roll out easily. Then proceed as in original recipe.

Makes approximately 1 dozen pieces

/ / /

Pita Bread
(Pocket Bread)

1 yeast cake or envelope dry
  yeast
1¼ cups warm water

3 cups wheat flour
1 tsp. salt
Vegetable oil as needed

Soak yeast in warm water (115°) for about 45 minutes. Sift in flour and salt and mix. Turn dough out onto a floured board and, moistening hands with oil, knead thoroughly, adding flour as needed. Divide dough into 6 pieces, kneading each piece well and form into a ball. Roll out on a floured board to make a 5-inch disk ¼ inch thick. Dredge pita disks lightly with flour, and place on a clean towel, and cover with another towel. Leave for 45 minutes, or until breads are 1½ times larger than their original size. Place on an oiled cookie sheet and bake in preheated 500° oven for 10 to 15 minutes. Bread will puff up and will soften once it has cooled off.

Makes 6 pieces

/ / /

Sesame-Seed Honey Bread

SPONGE MIXTURE:

2½ tbsp. dry yeast
6 cups warm water

½ cup honey
4 cups whole-grain wheat flour

4 cups all-purpose flour
1 cup wheat germ
1 cup bran
1 cup sesame seeds

½ cup sesame oil
2½ tbsp. salt
2 egg yolks beaten with 2 tbsp.
    water

In a nonmetallic bowl add ingredients for sponge mixture, mix, and let stand until mixture becomes foamy. Then beat 100 times with a wooden spoon. Cover with a damp cloth and set aside for 30 to 40 minutes. Punch down mixture, which will have risen, and add all other ingredients except egg yolks. Knead until smooth and elastic. Cover dough with damp cloth and let rise in a warm place until double in volume, about 30 minutes. Divide dough into 4 equal parts, shape, and place in greased loaf pans. Brush with egg yolk-water mixture, cover, and let rise for 15 to 20 minutes. Bake in preheated 350° oven for 20 to 30 minutes. Loaves are done if they sound hollow when tapped.

Makes 4 loaves

/ / /

Whole Wheat Bread

1 tbsp. dry yeast
2½ cups warm water
3 tbsp. honey

3 tbsp. sesame oil or other
    cooking oil
6 cups whole wheat flour
2 tsp. salt

Dissolve yeast in water (115°) and add honey and oil. Blend flour and salt, and sift into liquid mixture. Knead until smooth and elastic. Cover dough with a clean towel and allow to rise until double in size. Punch down dough, form into two loaves, and place in well-greased loaf pans. Let rise again to tops of pans and bake in preheated 350° oven for 30 minutes.

Makes 2 loaves

/ / /

Whole Wheat Crackers

1 cup whole wheat flour
¼ tsp. salt
¼ cup vegetable oil
3 to 4 tbsp. ice water

Sift flour and salt into oil in a bowl. Mix and add water, a little at a time. Dough should have texture of pie crust. Chill for 30 minutes or more. Roll out dough on a floured board until very thin. Using a pastry cutter, cut dough into squares, rectangles, or triangles. Place on an oiled cookie sheet and bake in preheated 350° oven for 10 to 15 minutes until crisp and lightly browned.

Makes approximately 1 dozen crackers

DESSERTS

Applesauce

2 sweet apples, peeled, cored, and quartered
⅓ cup water

Thinly slice apples and place in a small stainless-steel pan with the water. Bring to a boil, reduce heat, and simmer, covered, for approximately 5 minutes, or until apples are tender. Cool. Pour apples and liquid into a blender or food processor and blend to desired consistency.

3 or 4 child servings

/ / /

Baked Apples

1 red apple for each person, washed and cored
1 tbsp. seedless raisins each
1 pat of butter each

When coring apples take care not to cut through bottom. Fill center of each apple with raisins, cover with a pat of butter, and stand apples in an ovenproof dish with enough water to cover the bottom. Bake in preheated 350° oven for 1 hour, or until apples are cooked through.

For babies, mash apple and raisins after removing apple skin.

Serves 1

/ / /

Apple Gel

2 cups apple juice
1 envelope unflavored gelatin

Put ½ cup apple juice in a bowl and sprinkle with gelatin. Let stand for 1 minute. Put remaining apple juice in a saucepan and bring to a boil, then add to the gelatin mixture. Stir until gelatin is completely dissolved. Pour into a mold or individual serving dishes and refrigerate until firm.

Serves 4

/ / /

Apple Mist

1 small sweet apple, peeled and cored
⅓ cup apple juice
2 tbsp. cream

Slice apples, then cut slices in half. Put into a small saucepan with apple juice and simmer until apples are soft. Remove from heat and mash well. Add cream and mix with a wire whisk. Serve warm or cold.

1 child serving

/ / /

Homemade Apple Pie

FOR PASTRY:

1½ cups cake or all-purpose
    flour
½ tsp. baking powder
½ tsp. salt

⅓ to ½ cup shortening (butter
    or other fat)
¼ cup ice water
    (approximately)

FILLING:

4 apples, peeled, cored, and
    sliced
3 tsp. butter

Cinnamon (optional)

Sift flour, baking powder, and salt into a large bowl. Cut shortening into flour with a knife until the size of peas. Then mix with hands, breaking up shortening very lightly until ingredients are of a crumb-like consistency. Add ice water a little at a time until a firm dough is achieved. It is important not to add too much water. If mixture should become sticky, add a little more flour. Turn dough out onto a cold floured board or table, and divide into 2 pieces. With floured hands and rolling pin, roll out each piece until ½ inch thick. Fold in thirds and roll again. Repeat. Place dough in refrigerator for ½ hour, then roll out each piece until it is large enough to fit a 9-inch pie dish.

Grease pie dish, moisten edge of dish with water, and loosely lay one round of dough over dish. Gently press dough down into base and sides of dish and fill with apple slices. Dot with butter and sprinkle with cinnamon (if desired).

Roll out top crust, moisten edge of bottom crust with water, and cover pie with top layer. Trim off extra pastry, then pinch top and bottom layers of pastry together. Prick upper crust a couple of times with a fork. Place pie in preheated 450° oven for 12 minutes. Reduce heat to 350° and bake for 25 to 35 minutes more, or until crust is brown. (For a more golden and shiny crust, brush top with a mixture of milk and egg yolk before baking.)

Serves 4 to 6

/ / /

Poached Apples

4 green (pippin) apples
Juice of ½ lemon
⅔ cup fresh orange juice

2 tbsp. water
Pinch ground cinnamon

Wash apples, cut into quarters, and remove core and seeds. Slice segments thin and place in a lidded frying pan. Cover apples with lemon juice and all other ingredients. Cook over low heat, turning slices occasionally, until the apples are soft but not mushy. It is important to keep the apples covered to poach them except when turning them.

Serves 4

/ / /

Apple Strawberry Parfaits

2 envelopes unflavored gelatin
3 cups apple juice
3 cups sliced strawberries

Sprinkle both envelopes of gelatin over 1½ cups cold apple juice and let stand for 1 minute. Heat remaining juice to boiling point and add to gelatin mixture, stirring until gelatin is dissolved. Pour into an 8-inch-square baking dish and refrigerate until firm. Using a fork, break up gelatin into small pieces and put a spoonful into each of 6 parfait glasses. Follow with a layer of strawberries, another layer of gelatin, then more strawberries, ending with a top layer of gelatin.

For a special treat or occasion, either whipped cream or ice cream can be added as an extra layer or used as a topping.

Serves 6

/ / /

ABC (Apricots/Banana/Cream) Dessert

2 stewed apricots, puréed
½ ripe banana, peeled
1 tbsp. whipped cream

Mash banana to desired consistency, place in a small dish, and top with puréed apricots. Serve with a dollop of whipped cream.

1 child serving

/ / /

Cold Apricot Soup

1 lb. dried apricots
1 cup cream (or half-and-half)

Cover apricots with warm water and soak for 1 hour. Blend apricots and soaking water in a food processor or blender until puréed. Strain mixture through a sieve, stir in cream, and chill. Serve with a dollop of whipped cream.

Serves 4

/ / /

Broiled Banana

½ large ripe, but firm, banana
1 tsp. unsalted butter, melted
1 tsp. lime or lemon juice

Place unpeeled banana under preheated broiler, about 5 inches from the flame, for 10 minutes, turning fruit once. Remove from heat with tongs, peel and mash banana, and mash again to desired consistency with butter and lime or lemon juice.

1 child serving

/ / /

Banana Coconut Pudding

2 eggs
1 ripe banana, peeled and
    mashed
¼ cup grated coconut

¼ cup milk, half-and-half, or
    light cream
½ tsp. vanilla essence

In a mixing bowl, beat eggs. Add banana, coconut, milk, and vanilla essence, and stir ingredients until blended. Pour mixture into a small ovenproof casserole, then stand casserole in a larger pan almost filled with water. Place in preheated 350° oven and bake for 1 hour, or until set.

Serves 4

/ / /

Banana Raita

1 tsp. ghee (clarified butter, see page 251)
⅛ tsp. ground cardamom
1 ripe banana
¼ cup yogurt

In a frying pan melt ghee with cardamom over medium heat. Mash banana well and mix with yogurt. When ghee is melted and bubbling gently, add banana to pan and stir vigorously. To serve this dish warm, just cook until heated through; to serve cold, mix the ingredients well, then remove from heat and chill.

1 adult and 1 child serving

/ / /

Norwegian Birthday Cake

6 medium eggs
1 cup sugar
½ tsp. baking powder
1½ cups all-purpose flour

FOR FILLING:

2 packages frozen raspberries
Two 16-oz. cans raspberries

Two 8-oz. cartons cream,
    whipped
1 tsp. vanilla essence

Defrost frozen berries and strain all the raspberries, reserving juice. Beat eggs and sugar together with a hand mixer until very light. Mix baking powder with flour and sift into eggs and sugar, beat lightly until smooth, and pour mixture into a greased and floured round springform cake pan. Bake in preheated 350° oven for 45 minutes, or until a toothpick when inserted comes out clean. Place cake on a rack to cool, then turn out onto a plate. When cake is completely cool, cut in half horizontally, and soak both layers with all the reserved raspberry juice. (This part of the recipe may be made a day ahead. The cake should be covered and refrigerated until ready to finish.)

Cover bottom layer of cake with raspberries and cover generously with whipped cream flavored with vanilla essence. Top with second layer and cover with remaining whipped cream. Decorate with fresh berries, flowers, candles, or as desired.

Makes 10 or 12 servings

/ / /

Bread Pudding

2 cups stale bread, broken into
    pieces
2 cups milk
2 eggs, separated

3 tbsp. unsalted butter, melted
1 tsp. vanilla essence
⅓ cup raisins

Butter the sides and bottom of an ovenproof casserole and line with
bread pieces. Pour milk over the bread to soften and let stand for
15 minutes. Meanwhile, beat together egg yolks, melted butter, and
vanilla essence. Add mixture and raisins to bread and milk, and
stir to mix. Beat egg whites until stiff and fold into mixture lightly.
Preheat oven to 400°, set the casserole in a large pan half filled
with water, and bake for 1 hour.

Serves 4

/ / /

Cottage Cheese Pudding

½ cup milk, or more if mixture
    needs thinning
2 cups small-curd cottage
    cheese

Juice and grated peel of ¼
    lemon
¼ tsp. vanilla essence
½ tsp. ground cardamom

Put all ingredients in a blender or food processor, starting with the
milk. Blend until smooth. Pour into individual dishes or bowl and
refrigerate until set.

Serves 4

/ / /

Cranberry Cubes

3 cups cranberry juice
3 envelopes unflavored gelatin

Put 1½ cups cold cranberry juice in a large bowl and sprinkle with gelatin. Let stand for 1 minute. Meanwhile, heat remaining juice to boiling point. Add heated juice to gelatin mixture and stir until gelatin is completely dissolved. Pour into an 8-inch-square baking dish and chill until firm.

To serve, cut into 1-inch squares. This dessert is fun for children to decorate with fruits like mandarin orange segments, a slice of banana, pitted cherries or grapes, etc.

Serves 6

/ / /

Figs in Yogurt

6 fresh figs
¼ cup ground pistachios and
  almonds, well mixed
orange juice for marinade

1 cup plain yogurt, preferably
  homemade (see page 149)
1 tbsp. honey
¼ tsp. vanilla essence

Wash figs, cut off tops, and carefully stuff 1 teaspoon ground nuts into each fig. Stand figs in a dish approximately 4 inches deep and cover with orange juice. Marinate for 45 minutes, then remove from juice with a slotted spoon. Mix ¼ cup orange-juice marinade with yogurt, honey, and vanilla essence, and divide mixture among 6 small custard cups. Place a fig in each cup and chill until ready to serve.

Serves 6

/ / /

Fruit Compote

¼ lb. pitted dried prunes
¼ lb. pitted dried apricots
1 apple, peeled, cored, and diced
1 ripe pear, peeled, cored, and diced

Soak prunes and apricots overnight in a pan with enough water to cover. Using same water, bring fruit to a boil and add apple and pear. Return to heat and bring back to a boil, reduce heat a little, and cook until fruit is soft and most of the liquid has been absorbed. Stir occasionally to prevent sticking. Serve warm or cold, with a little milk if desired. Purée compote for babies without teeth; mash to coarser texture for older children.

Serves 4

/ / /

Fruit Custard

2 egg yolks
½ cup puréed fruit (banana, plums, pears, peaches, or combination
   of any two)
¼ cup whole milk
¼ tsp. vanilla essence

Beat egg yolks well, add fruit, milk, and vanilla essence, and continue to beat until smooth. With a dot of butter, lightly grease 2 custard cups, pour mixture into cups, and bake in preheated 350° oven for 30 minutes, or until set.

1 adult and 1 child serving

/ / /

Fresh Fruit Salad

1 small orange, peeled, seeded, and chopped (include juice)
1 apple, peeled, cored, and chopped
1 ripe banana, peeled and cut up
1 ripe pear, peeled, cored, and chopped

Put all ingredients in a bowl and mix well. For children, may be served with a little cold milk, if desired.

Serves 2

/ / /

Grape Divine

2 cups grape juice
1 envelope unflavored gelatin

Sprinkle gelatin over ½ cup of the grape juice in a bowl and let stand for 1 minute. Bring remaining juice to a boil and add to the gelatin mixture, stirring until gelatin is dissolved. Refrigerate in the bowl until mixture is the consistency of unbeaten egg whites. Using electric mixer, beat at high speed until jelled mixture triples in volume (about 10 minutes). Chill until set.

Serves 4

/ / /

Kiwi Kwiki

1 kiwi fruit, peeled and sliced crosswise
½ ripe banana, peeled
1 tbsp. vanilla ice cream

Cut kiwi slices again in half, and thinly slice banana. In a small dessert dish combine both fruits, saving two kiwi slices for decoration. Top with ice cream and finish with kiwi slices arranged like butterfly wings. An easy recipe to multiply to serve as many as you wish.

Serves 1

/ / /

Melon Berry Melba

¼ cup cranberry juice
¼ cup orange juice
1 cup fresh raspberries
2 cups cantaloupe balls

Freeze juices in ice cube tray, then lightly crush in blender. In 4 sherbet glasses divide up raspberries and cantaloupe balls, and drizzle crushed fruit ice over top. Serve immediately.

Serves 4

/ / /

Cold Melon Soup

¼ ripe cantaloupe, peeled and seeded
¼ cup orange juice
1 tbsp. plain yogurt

Cut cantaloupe into chunks and purée in a food processor. Add orange juice and yogurt, and blend until smooth. Chill well before serving. For a more elegant dessert, add small melon balls and/or a dollop of whipped cream and top with a sprig of mint.

1 adult and 1 child serving

/ / /

Orange Cloud

½ cup orange juice
1 envelope unflavored gelatin
½ cup water
1 cup cold milk

Put orange juice in a bowl, sprinkle with gelatin, and let stand for 1 minute. Bring ½ cup water to a boil, pour over gelatin mixture, and stir until gelatin is completely dissolved. Slowly add cold milk and stir well. Pour into a mold or individual dessert cups and refrigerate until set.

4 child servings

/ / /

Orange Soufflé

3 eggs, separated
1 cup cream
Juice of 3 oranges, seeds removed
1 tsp. vanilla essence

Beat egg whites until they form soft peaks, and beat cream until stiff. In a bowl mix orange juice, egg yolks, and vanilla essence, and whisk with a fork. *Gently* add egg whites and cream and fold all ingredients together until mixed. Keep chilled until ready to serve.

Serves 4

/ / /

Norwegian Pancakes

2 eggs
1½ cups milk
¾ cup all-purpose flour

¼ tsp. cardamom
Vegetable oil for cooking
Blueberry jam for topping*

Beat eggs in a bowl, add milk, and sift in flour and cardamom. Beat all ingredients lightly until a smooth thin batter is achieved. Heat 1 teaspoon oil in a small omelet or nonstick frying pan until almost smoking. Add just enough batter to coat bottom of pan, rotating pan to spread the batter very thinly. Shake pan gently to prevent sticking and when pancake is brown on one side, flip over with a spatula to cook the other side. (This should take only a few seconds.) Turn out onto a warm plate and serve immediately with jam.

Makes 8 to 12 pancakes, depending on size

*For variations, fresh berries, peaches, pears, applesauce, sliced bananas, or ice cream for a special treat, can be substituted.

/ / /

Peachy Pudding

2 cups peach nectar
1 cup vanilla ice cream
1 envelope unflavored gelatin

Place ½ cup of the peach nectar in a large bowl and sprinkle with gelatin. Set aside while heating remaining nectar in a small saucepan. Combine gelatin mixture with heated nectar and stir until gelatin is dissolved. Chill until partially jelled, approximately 1 to 2 hours, then place in a blender with ice cream and blend until well mixed. Pour into an attractive dish and chill until firm.

Serves 4

/ / /

Pear Surprise

2 ripe sweet pears, peeled, halved, and cored
1 mandarin orange, peeled, seeded, and cut in pieces (or small can mandarin orange segments), chilled
4 tbsp. plain yogurt or whipped cream

Trim a very small slice from the round side of each pear half, so it will sit level on a plate. Fill each hollow with 1 tablespoonful mandarin oranges, and cover with yogurt or whipped cream.

Serves 4

/ / /

Persimmon with Grapes

1 ripe persimmon
5 black grapes

Cut persimmon in half and remove center pith. Scoop out flesh with a spoon and cut into small pieces. Halve grapes and remove any seeds. Arrange in a small dish and serve with half-and-half, cream, or vanilla ice cream.

Serves 1

/ / /

Stewed Plums

12 ripe sweet plums
½ cup water
1 tsp. vanilla essence

Wash plums, cut in half, and remove pits. Put water in a saucepan, add plums, cover, and simmer until tender, approximately 15 minutes. Drain liquid from plums and save (for Plum Yum, next recipe). Purée plums in a food processor, blender, or food mill, adding vanilla essence. Cool a little before serving.

If plums are too tart for your baby, add a little mashed banana or papaya to the purée.

4 child servings

/ / /

Plum Yum

½ cup plum syrup (saved from stewed plums, preceding recipe)
¼ tsp. lemon juice
½ tsp. vanilla essence
1½ tsp. arrowroot, potato flour, or cornstarch

Mix syrup, lemon juice, and vanilla essence in a small saucepan
and bring to a boil. In a cup mix arrowroot with a little water to a
smooth thin consistency. Add slowly to boiling syrup, stirring constantly, until syrup is clear and thickened. Remove from heat and
let it cool and thicken. Serve with milk.

2 to 3 child servings

/ / /

Raspberry Tarte

¼ cup fresh raspberries
Pastry shell (following recipe)
1 tbsp. vanilla-flavored whipped cream

Make pastry shell according to directions and let cool. Rinse raspberries and drain until dry, then fill shell. Top with whipped cream
just before serving.

Makes 1 tart

/ / /

Pastry Shells

1 tbsp. corn oil
2 tsp. cold water
1½ tbsp. whole wheat flour
2 tbsp. all-purpose flour

Beat oil and water together with a fork, then sift in flours, and mix until a pliable dough is formed. Grease individual cupcake or pie tins 2½ inches in diameter. Divide dough into 4 pieces and press 1 piece into each tin, using thumb to make a thin even crust. Bake in preheated 375° oven for 10 to 15 minutes until shells are a light golden brown. Cool, unmold, and fill with berries, applesauce, creamed chicken, etc.

Makes 4 shells

/ / /

Rice Pudding

2 cups milk
2 eggs
1 tsp. vanilla essence
1 tbsp. vegetable oil
½ cup raisins

½ tsp. each cinnamon and
grated lemon rind (optional)
1 cup cooked rice (white or
brown)

With a fork, mix together milk, eggs, vanilla essence, and oil, add raisins (plus cinnamon and lemon rind, if desired), and pour mixture over rice in an ovenproof dish. Place dish in a larger pan half filled with water and bake in preheated 300° oven until milk is absorbed but pudding is still creamy (about 1 to 1½ hours). Stir occasionally during cooking.

Serves 4

/ / /

Rice and Apricot Pudding

½ cup cooked rice
½ cup cooked apricots with liquid
1 tsp. vanilla essence
Milk (optional)

Put rice, apricots, and vanilla in a food processor fitted with steel blade, or in a blender, and process until puréed. If a creamier consistency is desired, add a little milk while blending. Other fruits, such as cooked prunes, plums, or pineapple, can be substituted for the apricots.

2 or 3 child servings

/ / /

Summer Delight

½ cup cubed ripe melon or
    watermelon
½ cup cubed fresh or canned
    pineapple

½ cup diced pear
½ cup diced apple
¼ cup orange juice

Combine all ingredients in a bowl and toss with orange juice. Chill for at least 1 hour before serving.

Serves 4

/ / /

Strawberry Banana Mold

1 bar white agar*
1½ cups of water
1½ cups apple juice

1 package frozen strawberries,
*   thawed and drained*
1 banana, sliced

Break agar into pieces and soak in 1½ cups water in a saucepan for about 10 minutes. Purée half the strawberries in a blender with a little of the apple juice. Meanwhile, bring agar mixture to a boil. Add puréed strawberries, reduce heat, and simmer for 10 minutes, stirring frequently, then add remaining apple juice. Arrange remaining strawberries and sliced banana in the bottom of a mold lightly coated with vegetable oil, and gently pour puréed mixture over the fruit. Refrigerate until firm, usually 1 to 2 hours. Serve unmolded.

Serves 4

---

*Agar is a gelatin derived from seaweed. It contains many minerals and is beneficial as a laxative. This tasteless jelling agent can be used in place of animal gelatin. As well as being available in bar form, agar also comes in flakes or granules. Basic proportions are 3½ cups liquid (water and/or fruit juice) to 2 tablespoons flakes or 1 tablespoon granules. For a softer jell, use 4 cups liquid.

/ / /

Strawberry Fruit Soup

1 box strawberries, washed and hulled
4 tbsp. lemon juice
2 tbsp. sugar, dissolved in a little hot water
2 cups plain yogurt (see page 149 for homemade)

Blend strawberries, lemon juice, and sugar in a food processor or blender until smooth. Pour into a bowl and stir in yogurt. Serve chilled.

Serves 4

/ / /

Tropical Treat

1 mango, peeled and pitted
¼ cup cream, whipped

Cut mango into small pieces and press through a sieve or food grinder. Gently fold in whipped cream and serve immediately.

1 adult and 1 child serving

/ / /

Yogurt Ambrosia

½ ripe banana
3 tbsp. chopped fresh papaya
2 tbsp. plain yogurt (for homemade see page 149)
5 drops lemon juice

Finely chop or mash banana together with the papaya and fold into yogurt. Add lemon juice and blend well.

1 child serving

FRUIT AND MILK DRINKS

Apricot Avocado Zest

12-oz. can apricot nectar
½ cup milk
1 small ripe avocado, peeled,
   pitted, and cut in chunks

Combine all ingredients in a blender and process until smooth.
Serves 2

/ / /

Apricot Breakfast Shake

1 cup apricot nectar
1 cup plain yogurt
1 ripe banana, peeled and cut in chunks
3 ice cubes, cracked

Combine all ingredients in a blender and process until smooth and
fluffy.
Serves 2

/ / /

Banana Strawberry Smoothie

1 ripe banana, peeled and cut in chunks
1 cup strawberries, washed and hulled
1 cup ice-cold milk

Combine all ingredients in a blender, process until smooth, and serve.

Serves 2

/ / /

Hawaiian Chiffon

4 cups pineapple juice
1 ripe banana, peeled and cut in chunks
Large handful ground almonds

Process well in a blender and serve immediately.

Serves 4

/ / /

Minty Treat

4 cups orange juice, well chilled
2 ripe bananas, peeled and cut in chunks
½ tsp. dried mint leaves

Place all ingredients in a blender and process well. Serve immediately.

Serves 4

/ / /

Orange Milk Whip

½ cup milk
½ cup orange juice

Mix in a blender or food processor for 10 seconds. Serve immediately.

1 child serving

/ / /

Papaya Shake

1 papaya, peeled, pitted, and cut in half
1 pint orange sherbet
2 cups milk

Put all ingredients into a blender and process until smooth and frothy.

Serves 4

/ / /

Raspberry Tofu Smoothie

½ pint raspberries, rinsed (or other berries)
8 oz. tofu
3 ripe bananas, peeled and cut in chunks

Process in a blender until smooth and serve immediately.

Serves 3 to 4

/ / /

Tropical Cooler

¼ cup dried apricots
½ cup warm water
1 medium-ripe banana

1 mango, peeled and pitted
2 tsp. lemon juice
12 ice cubes, cracked

Soak apricots in warm water for 10 minutes, then place in a blender with water and add banana, mango, and lemon juice. Cover and process until smooth. Remove center of blender cover and gradually add cracked ice, blending at high speed. Continue to blend for 2 minutes until drink is smooth.

Serves 4

STOCKS AND SAUCES

Chicken Stock or Broth

Carcass and leftover meat from
    roast chicken
2 stalks celery, washed and
    halved
2 carrots, scrubbed and cut
    into thirds

1 onion, peeled and quartered
1 bay leaf
1 tsp. salt
Water to cover

Place all ingredients in a large pot and bring to a boil. Reduce heat and cook at low simmer for approximately 2 hours. When cool enough, strain broth, saving liquid and chicken meat, and discard everything else.

/ / /

Vegetable Soup or Stock

2 large potatoes, scrubbed and
  cubed
1 cup shredded carrots
1 cup chopped celery (include
  leaves)
1 cup beet or turnip tops,
  parsley, or other leafy
  vegetable, chopped

1 onion, peeled and quartered
1 clove garlic, peeled
1 bay leaf
1 tsp. dried herbs (mixed, or as
  desired)
1½ quarts cold water

Put all ingredients in a large pot, bring to a boil, reduce heat, and
simmer for 30 minutes. To serve as soup, remove bay leaf and
purée briefly in batches in a blender. Serve warm. To serve as a
clear broth or stock, strain out chopped vegetables through a sieve
or cheesecloth. If not used immediately, store in refrigerator and
reheat before using.

/ / /

Fresh Herb Sauce

2 tbsp. cold water
3 tbsp. lemon juice
2 tbsp. fish broth (optional)
Dash white pepper

½ cup hot (170°) melted
  unsalted butter
2 tsp. fresh tarragon, basil,
  dill, or chives, minced

In a small enamel saucepan put water, lemon juice, fish broth (if
desired), and pepper, and bring to a boil. Pour into a food processor
or blender and with machine running, pour in hot melted butter a
little at a time, but take no more than 20 seconds. Process for 5
seconds and add minced herb of your choice. Process 5 seconds
more and serve.

Makes 4 servings

/ / /

Marinara Sauce

1 clove garlic, peeled
¼ cup olive oil
2-lb. can tomatoes

1 tsp. salt
½ tsp. oregano
1 tsp. chopped parsley

Gently sauté garlic in heated oil for a few minutes. Meanwhile, purée tomatoes in a blender or food processor and add to oil with all other ingredients, removing garlic clove if desired. Cook slowly for 45 minutes, stirring occasionally. May be made ahead and frozen for later use.

/ / /

Tomato Sauce

3 tbsp. olive oil
3 cloves garlic, peeled and
    lightly crushed
1 large onion, peeled and
    chopped
28-oz. can tomatoes

28-oz. can tomato purée
Two 6-oz. cans tomato paste
1 tbsp. each oregano and basil,
    crushed
1 tsp. salt

Heat oil in a skillet, add garlic and onion, and sauté until onion is golden. Chop tomatoes for a few seconds in a food processor, and add to onion and garlic with all remaining ingredients. Stir well, bring to a boil, then reduce heat and simmer for 15 to 20 minutes. Cooked ground meat and/or sliced sautéed mushrooms may be added, if desired.

This sauce freezes well and can be kept in sealed containers for use as needed.

/ / /

White Sauce

1½ tbsp. butter
1½ tbsp. all-purpose flour
1 cup liquid (equal parts broth and milk, or 1 cup milk, or 1 cup chicken or vegetable broth)

In a heavy-bottomed saucepan (do not use aluminum), melt butter over *low heat*. Blend in flour a little at a time, stirring constantly with a wooden spoon until butter and flour bubble. Cook for 2 minutes, still stirring, until mixture is smooth. Remove from heat and set aside for a minute until bubbling has stopped. Add liquid and beat vigorously with a wire whip until sauce is completely blended and without lumps. Return to moderate heat and stir with whip until sauce comes to a boil. Simmer for 1 minute and cover until ready to serve.

For thinner sauce, use 1 tablespoon each flour and butter, and 1 cup liquid.

For thicker sauce, use 2 tablespoons each flour and butter, and 1 cup liquid.

This basic sauce may be used in many ways and is especially good with grated cheddar cheese added, or sautéed sliced mushrooms. Serve over fish, chicken, eggs, and vegetables.

/ / /

Tahini Dressing

½ cup tahini*
½ cup lemon juice
1 clove garlic, minced
2 tbsp. minced fresh parsley

2 tbsp. olive oil
Dash pepper
Salt (optional)

*Tahini is sesame-seed paste, available in health-food or Middle Eastern grocery stores.

Place all ingredients in a blender or food processor and process until smooth. If necessary, add a little water to thin to desired consistency.

References

Composition of Foods—Raw, Processed, Prepared (Agricultural Handbook No. 8), by Bernice K. Watt and Annabel L. Merrill. Washington, D.C.: U.S. Department of Agriculture, Agricultural Research Service, 1963.

Diet Manual Massachusetts General Hospital. Boston: Little, Brown, 1976.

Essentials of Nutrition and Diet Therapy by Sue Rodwell Williams. St. Louis: The C. V. Mosby Company, 1974.

Maternal and Child Nutrition: Assessment and Counseling by Jill S. Slattery, et al., eds. New York: Appleton-Century-Crofts, 1979.

Nutrition in Infancy and Childhood by Peggy L. Pipes. St. Louis: The C. V. Mosby Company, 1977.

Pediatric Nutrition Handbook. Evanston, Ill.: American Academy of Pediatrics, 1979.

Recommended Dietary Allowances. Washington, D.C.: Food and Nutrition Board, National Academy of Sciences, National Research Council, Revised 1980.

We are indebted to the following authors from whose books we have adapted recipes and cooking methods for the special purposes of *The Baby Cookbook:*

Atwater, Maxine. *Natural Foods Cookbook.* Concord, Calif.: Nitty Gritty Productions, 1972.

Cottrell, Edith Young. *The Oats, Peas, Beans and Barley Cookbook.* Santa Barbara, Calif.: Woodbridge Press, 1974.

Hunter, Beatrice Trum. *The Natural Foods Cookbook*. New York: Simon & Schuster, 1961.

Wilson, Ellen Gibson. *A West African Cook Book*. New York: M. Evans, 1971.

Zane, Eva. *Middle Eastern Cookery*. San Francisco: 101 Productions, 1974.

General Index

Recipe Index

Special recipes for babies and toddlers are entered in this index in **boldface type**.